ICART

ICART

BY S. MICHAEL SCHNESSEL

INTRODUCTION BY
KATHARINE M. McCLINTON

STUDIO VISTA
London

FOR

Louis and Fanny

A Studio Vista Book published by
Cassell& Collier Macmillan Publishers Ltd.
35 Red Lion Square, London WC1R 4SG
and at Sydney, Auckland, Toronto, Johannesburg,
an affiliate of
Macmillan Publishing Co., Inc.,
New York

First published in the USA by Clarkson N. Potter ,Inc., 1976
One Park Avenue, New York, N.Y. 10016
First published in Great Britain by Studio Vista 1976
Printed in the United States of America

ISBN 0 289.70761.7

Front cover: Grande Eve *(Eve and the Serpent).*
Back cover: Mimi Pinson, *drypoint and etching, 1927.* © *1927, 1954 by Fanny Icart.*
Title page: Coursing II, *drypoint and etching, 1929, 25 x 15½.*
Fig. 62: Dame aux Camelias © *1927, 1953 by Fanny Icart.*
Fig. 85: Poupée Moderne © *1926, 1953 by Fanny Icart.*
Fig. 92: Thaïs © *1927, 1954 by Fanny Icart.*
Fig. 102: Fumée © *1926, 1953 by Fanny Icart.*

Printed in the United States of America

Color separations
by Bengal Graphics

CONTENTS

Fig. 1. *Dans les Branches* (The Swing), drypoint and etching, 1928, 13½ x 19. (Collection of the Library of Congress)

INTRODUCTION *by Katharine M. McClinton*

WHEN LOUIS ICART ARRIVED IN PARIS IN 1907, PARIS WAS THE UNCONTESTED INTERNATIONAL center of art and beauty, personifying the joyous insouciant life of "La Belle Epoque." The Eiffel Tower had been built in 1889 and the Moulin Rouge, with its red sails cutting the sky of Montmartre, was the scene of gorgeous displays and spicy shows. Montmartre was flourishing as the literary and artistic center of Paris. The famous restaurant Maxim's had also opened its doors at the turn of the century. Then there was the theatre world—Monday nights at the Opéra were still elegant, with the men in full dress sitting on the *parterre* while the women sat in the boxes flashing with jewels and décolleté gowns from Worth and Paquin. The queens of the *demimonde* brushed shoulders with duchesses and later sat on banquettes at the after-theatre restaurants such as the Café de la Paix. The Théâtre Sarah Bernhardt had opened in 1900 and there was the Opéra Comique that performed such musical dramas as *Manon* and *Werther* by Massenet, *Carmen* by Bizet, and *Madame Butterfly* by Puccini. There were also various kinds of revues and cabarets including those at the Chat Noir and, of course, the famous Folies Bergère.

Modern Paris with its bright lights, its spacious squares, its fashionable Faubourg Saint-Germain, its working class districts, its huge markets, its schools, and its transport system had already been built as a result of the planning of Baron Haussmann. This was also the end of "La Belle Epoque" of the arts. The decorative arts were emerging from the vague and capricious Art Nouveau style and the idealized sentiment of beauty expressed as elegance. Emile Gallé was still working at the end of the century but died in 1905, and Lalique, who had been designing genius-inspired jewelry, began to work in glass, creating vases, lamps, mirrors, fountains, as well as the flacons for the perfumes of Coty and other perfumers, and the colorful glass ceiling of Maxim's café.

In 1907 Picasso's *Demoiselles d'Avignon* initiated the Cubist revolution. Also Futurism, Fauvism, and exhibitions of African Art all had their influence on French painting at this time.

The turning point was in 1909 with the first performances of Serge Diaghilev's Ballet Russes at the Théâtre des Champs Elysées, with its brilliant color stage sets and costumes by Léon Bakst. *Cleopatra* was the first ballet presented in Paris in 1909. The scenery and costumes were in vibrant colors with an orange backdrop, vivid blue floor, and a sky-blue curtain. The dancers, including Anna Pavlova and Léonide Massine, were in multicolored costumes spangled with gold. *Schéhérazade*, in 1910, was even more striking with its contrasts of the violent complementary colors, red and green. The success of the Ballet Russes continued with the performances of *The Firebird, The Spectre of the Rose, Petrouchka, L'Après-midi d'un Faune* with Nijinsky, *The Rite of Spring,* and *Le Coq d'Or.* They lasted until the outbreak of the First World War in 1914.

By 1909 Parisians also were becoming aware of Futurism and the Fauve artists, Matisse, Derain, Vlaminck, Van Dongen, and Braque, were producing two-dimensional representations. Paul Poiret, the designer of *haute couture,* was a histrionic personality in Paris from the year 1910. Poiret created clothes for great ladies, "cocottes," actresses, and variety stars such as Mistinguett. For his designs he employed the artists Paul Iribe, Raoul Dufy, and Georges Lepape, contemporaries of Louis Icart.

The war in 1914 did not end the progress of the arts; instead it probably aided in producing the change from Art Nouveau to Art Deco, which, however, did not come into full blossom until the 1925 Exposition des Arts Décoratifs, which had been delayed because of the war.

Between the end of the war and the 1920s Louis Icart had become so successful that he was able to devote most of his time to painting and etching. The popularity of Icart's etchings reached its height in this era of Art Deco. He has become the symbol of the epoch. Yet, although Icart gives us a picture of Paris life in the 1920s and 1930s, he worked in his own style, derived principally from the study of eighteenth-century French painting, and he lived outside the fashionable artistic movements of the time. However, even though Icart was not completely sympathetic to the art and life of the era, he did give us a more complete picture of Paris in the 1920s and 1930s than any other painter of the time. Paris is a series of pictures and Icart has painted them all—the life and scenes that he saw around him in his daily life. Icart's etchings of Paris street scenes are as popular today as when the etchings were first produced. There is not only the nostalgia for the traveler who visited Paris in the 1920s and 1930s, but the tourist in Paris today can see the same scenes. The architectural landmarks—the Eiffel Tower, the Arc de Triomphe, Place Vendôme, the Opéra, Notre Dame, and the Basilica of Sacré-Coeur—are all there, unchanged. One can still shop at the bookstalls on the Left Bank. There are the flower sellers with bouquets and flowers in pots, the chestnut vendors and fruit vendors in Les Halles and the Sunday bird market near Notre Dame. Icart pictures Montmartre at the time when he had his studio there. We see the little village of Old World streets, of tiny houses, and small gardens which had a character of provincial quietude. From the window of Icart's studio spread a panoramic view over the roofs of Paris, the Cathedral of Notre Dame, and the Eiffel Tower. In the etching *Mimi Pinson,* back cover, Icart re-creates this view. Icart has recorded these scenes of Paris for the time when they will be no more.

Other etchings bring us the excitement of Paris life in the Art Deco period. Icart depicts jazzy scenes at a typical Paris bar as well as the fêtes and Mardi Gras. However, we see no Art Deco zigzags or streaks of lightning in Icart's interpretation.

Art Deco was a fashion directed almost exclusively toward women. It applied to the rooms they used and the objects that surrounded them. Icart paints these frivolities with grace and feminine artistry, using the rounding spiral curves and soft colors of early Art Deco. His etchings include flowers, fountains, gazelles, butterflies, doves, swans and other feathered creatures, and the straining racing greyhounds. In the Coursing Series, the etching *Vitesse* (Speed) is especially reminiscent of Art Deco. Speed was an important characteristic of Art Deco; it found visual expression in streamlining, and contours were designed to go with the backward direction of the wind, giving the impression of flight as in horizontal streaks or lines. Speed and the force of the flowing line are seen in the Icart etching *Pur-sang*. The diagonal of the horse's head, the flowing mane, the extended nostrils and open mouth, and the lines of the rider all express strain and speed. The graceful galloping carrousel horse in the etching *A la Fête* (Mardi Gras) moves in Art Deco rhythm, as does the composition of the dark horse and figure in the etching *Jeunesse*.

Art Deco textures tended to be smooth, and curves were chaste, with a feeling of elegance which Icart captures in his work. Colors such as blue, grey, and inky black were characteristic of Art Deco, although Icart also favored pale pinks, from flesh to coral, and orchid. There was a vogue for outdoor life in the 1920s and people took to the beach and the tennis court readily. The theme of tennis was not only popular in the graphic arts, but also in textiles and in sculpture, especially in the small bronze and ivory figures. Icart used the tennis theme in one of his etchings.

Art Deco was a period of perfection of workmanship and this factor in Icart's work related him to the period. He was an expert craftsman and aimed for perfection in his etching technique. Art Deco was also a smart and sophisticated style. Icart surrounded himself with rich materials, fine furniture, Chinese lacquer screens, and other luxuries. This refinement of taste and the luxury with which he lived linked him to the opulent spirit of the times. In his pictures Icart tended to be romantic and flowery rather than stylish. His beautiful nudes are in poses so traditional yet so contemporary Art Deco. While much of Art Deco was conservative, such as the furniture of Paul Follot and that of Maurice Dufrene, which related to the Louis XVI period, there were changes that made it modish. Icart kept to the traditional, as did the decoration in the Provinces. In his home and in his etchings Icart depicts no Art Deco furniture. Instead we see eighteenth-century Louis XV desks and chairs. This is the elegance of the eighteenth century, not the smart "chic" of Art Deco.

In 1932, when Louis Icart was at the height of his career and the paintings "les visions blanches" were exhibited in America, I was the art critic on the now-defunct Scripps-Howard San Diego *Sun*. In my position as an art critic, I ignored Icart's exhibition in Los Angeles as did many others in art. However, I no longer look at his works with the eyes of a critic, but with the eyes of a collector, and it is difficult not to be drawn into the enchantment of Icart's dream world.

"*Et qui chantassent les plaisirs, puisque après tout, il y a des plaisirs.*" Audiberti, de l'Académie Mallarmé. In this volume Michael Schnessel has not only caught the enchantment of Icart's paintings and etchings, but he accepts Icart on his own terms—a serious artist but also a Frenchman always interested and willing to please the public in order to provide himself with the luxuries that he required as a cultured gentleman.

Schnessel has had access to Icart's personal papers and has talked with Icart's family and friends. The book is carefully researched and well written, and, although other books may be published, it is my guess that this book will remain the definitive volume.

Fig. 2. *Don Juan*, drypoint and etching, 1928, 14 x 21.

THE DECADES BETWEEN THE TWO WORLD WARS BROUGHT A PERSISTENT FRENCHMAN INTO THE American boudoir. He was there to delight, to tease, to fill the room with beauty, to evoke a wistful smile. His etchings of beautiful women, which graced homes throughout the country, epitomized the American perception of French "chic."

Icart held a firm grip on the popular decorative art market during the 1920s and 1930s, but with the approach of World War II, his etchings, victims of the ebbing tide of changing fashion, were relegated to storerooms and basements. Originally scheduled for the oblivion met by many of the popular arts of that era, Icart's etchings have, in recent years, made an agreeable reappearance, and they have quickly recaptured the heart of an eager, receptive public.

My first introduction to Louis Icart came during the summer of 1972 when I purchased a faded and mildewed copy of his 1928 etching *Don Juan* (Fig. 2) at a country house auction. My reasons for the purchase were no more than an admiration for the work, for the look of hapless innocence on the face of the young heroine, for the dash and vigor of the swordsman, who defends his lady with a verve that makes Errol Flynn look clumsy.

My instinctive writer's curiosity led me to investigate this mysterious artist. What little information I could find in libraries eventually directed me to a catalog published by the Louis Icart Society, a document replete with photographs of the other Icart treasures that would perhaps await me at future auctions. Within a short time I was an insatiable collector and soon discovered that I was by no means the first to find joy in the works of Louis Icart. In recent months I have become acquainted with collectors who have been accumulating Icart's works for many years. I have even met some older Icart fanciers who have been collecting his creations since they were first issued.

It is just this "collectibility" of Icart's etchings which partly explains their revival today. A collectible commodity must be available in enough quantity to generate a contagious enthusiasm. The act of collecting is, after all, a competitive activity. Originally, Icart etchings were produced in quantities large enough to satisfy the needs of the popular market. Buyers would select the etchings they wished from plentiful supplies at their local gallery or from their merchants' illustrated catalogs. If the desired etching were not in stock, a shipment from France would be due to arrive within a few weeks.

Today's Icart market is abundant with challenge. Buyers must depend on whatever they can find of a commodity that has suffered two decades of neglect. As a result, pieces that were originally produced in limited quantities are now more scarce than ever, and prices in the tight Icart collectors' world have seen a concomitant increase.

After sufficient quantity, variety is another basic essential of collectibility. Icart was a vigorous, prolific artist who did not deny his eager public. His individual creations number into the thousands, and the impressions obtained from each individual etching plate ranged from ten pieces to over a thousand. Despite the damaging effects of a major world war, and political and social changes, enough etchings have survived to meet the needs of a growing contemporary market.

But surely collectibility alone is hardly enough reason to explain the Icart revival. While he was among the first to produce "bedroom etchings," a term applied with hostility by certain critics, Icart was not the only producer of such pictures. The vogue for sensual images of languid ladies encouraged dozens of artists to supply similar works for the decorative picture trade. Icart's etchings, however, stand far above his imitators' in quality. His *demoiselles* are as French as the Champs-Elysées or the Moulin Rouge. The artist's comprehensive understanding of the graphic arts resulted in works that show great technical expertise. And, added to these qualities is a unique sense of humor that is appreciated by his loyal following.

This volume will attempt to convey to the reader a sense of his style and wit. It will examine and explain those features that make Icart's etchings so appealing to so many people. But while the etchings are the most ubiquitous features of his output, there are several other facets of his life and career that will be examined here. In his homeland Icart was admired as an oil painter, cartoonist, and book illustrator. His striking oils, which show reflections of many masters, and which are at the same time uniquely his own, reveal a side of his talent that is not always seen in the etchings. Icart's cartoons, which appeared in several French magazines, reveal a taste for social and political satire unseen in other works. Most surprising are the bizarre, often brutal, illustrations created for many of his limited edition *livres d'artistes*. These fine books, illustrated by autographic media, such as etching or lithograph, as opposed to photomechanical processes of reproduction, were bought by a small coterie of French collectors and have been seen in the United States only rarely. Some of the works he created for these books will be illustrated here in hopes of illuminating Icart's prodigious talent in a wide range of mediums.

Through this study of Icart's life and works I also seek to convey at least a portion of his gigantic personality to the reader. After a biographical chapter, which will hopefully dispel many of the myths that have circulated about Icart due to lack of sufficient printed information, the book will discuss his work by medium in separate chapters: etchings, oil paintings, watercolors, and limited edition books. Icart's other works, such as lithographs, menus, and advertisements, are grouped in a separate chapter.

Many of Icart's works are mentioned in passing in the biographical material, but more detailed discussion of those particular works may be found in the appropriate chapters following the biography. Only those etchings, paintings, or *livres d'artistes* that are representative of an entire group or that mark turning points in Icart's career are discussed in depth in the biographical material. Titles of works are given in French first, then English. The English title is not always a literal translation, however.

The two appendixes are designed to aid collectors and future researchers in locating examples of Icart's works. They include a listing of etchings copyrighted in the United States, giving the titles, publication dates, dimensions, and edition size when available, and a listing of trade books and *livres d'artistes* containing Icart's illustrations, giving all pertinent details about the editions.

Finally, a glossary has been included to define those technical terms or foreign words which would be tedious to define within the body of the text. In general, however, French terms are parenthetically translated into English upon first mention.

The illustrative material selected to accompany the text is meant to provide a generous sampling of works that typify Louis Icart's talents in various mediums. It is by no means possible to include here all the works created by this prolific artist, but I have taken care to use photographs that represent the finest examples of his output as well as those that typify an entire body of works.

The biographical information gathered here has come from disparate sources: from personal papers found in the Icart home in Montmartre; from contemporary newspaper and magazine articles; and from personal recollections of family members, friends, neighbors, and business associates. Many aspects of Icart's life, however, are doomed to remain a mystery. Only a few days before her death, Fanny Icart asked her husband's close friend, Manuel Robbe *fils,* to burn several boxes of mementos, letters, photographs, and documents. In a bizarre ceremony, M Robbe did her bidding on the upper terrace of the Icart home in Montmartre. Puzzled and troubled, he watched solemnly as several decades of memories were devoured by flames.

This work will, I hope, answer many questions about Louis Icart, although future researchers will surely discover additional facts of importance. Regardless, Icart will stand firmly on the strength of his talent. His temporary neglect, a small matter of two decades, will be forgotten by future generations, who will, I hope, be familiar with his name and his work, and realize his important role in the French decorative *and* fine arts of the early decades of this century.

ACKNOWLEDGMENTS

IF I AM GUILTY OF A CLICHÉ WHEN I SAY I COULD NOT HAVE DONE IT ALONE, THEN SO BE IT.
Creating this study of Louis Icart's life and work was not unlike assembling a puzzle—an international one, at that—and without the dedicated assistance of numerous persons, this book might never have materialized.

I first wish to thank Mme Reine Bénac, daughter of Louis and Fanny Icart. I am grateful for the many memories that she so graciously shared with me, and, even more important, for her unfailing confidence in my ability to prepare a thorough, objective portrayal of her father's work and life. To her husband, Henri Bénac, I offer my gratitude for his insistence on detail and accuracy, as well as his help and trust. Lastly, I thank them both for their ardent support during periods of crisis, in hopes that this work lives up to their every expectation.

Next I wish to thank M Pierre Landolt, whose kindness and generosity have helped to make this volume as complete as it is. By permitting me to work daily in his Paris home, the former residence of Louis and Fanny Icart, I obtained access to the hundreds of papers, artworks, and letters that have served as the basis of this volume.

Additionally I wish to thank the other friends and co-workers of Louis Icart for their recollections, and for giving me access to various materials—most notably the Taylor Foundation in Paris for permitting me to photograph the Icart works in their possession; to Mme Elise Mariaud whose personal anecdotes about Louis and Fanny Icart have greatly enriched this work; to Manuel Robbe *fils,* Claude Draeger, and

Michel Kieffer for their valuable insight into the processes of publishing, *gravures,* and the *livre d'artiste;* to the staff of Galeries Henaut for their helpful recollections on the exporting of Icart etchings to the United States; to the staff of S.P.A.D.E.M.; to Marie-Louise Arlabosse for her great help (and that important tape recorder); to Denis Milhau, Conservateur du Musée des Augustins; to R. C. Kenedy, Assistant Keeper of the Library, Victoria and Albert Museum; to the Service de Documentation Photographique de la Réunion des Musées Nationaux, Paris; to the Wallace Collection, London; to my friend Louis Pavagheau *fils* for his kind efforts on my behalf; and a very special thanks to Constance Konold for her diligent research assistance, for putting up with a crazy author, and for being just plain wonderful.

On American shores the list is even longer, and my thanks are equally vigorous. First, to my literary agent, James Kery, of Eclectic House, I offer my sincerest gratitude for his confidence, patience, and diligent efforts. The success of this book is due in no small part to his literary expertise and helpful consultation and advice. Secondly, to my business partner, Nick Procaccino, whose research, along with frequent encouragement, worked in concert to help me continue when things became difficult. Next, to Ellen Winans and Jane Saul of Graphics, Etc., in Provincetown, Massachusetts, whose assistance and belief in my project will never be forgotten. I wish to thank Sonia Charif of Déjà Vu, New York City, whose insightful observations on Icart's work were of great help. To Jonathan Talbot for his knowledge of graphic arts. To George Theofiles for an important addition of detail. To Howard Hartman, a healthy thank-you for his finely detailed research on early aviation and Icart. And, also, to Anton Schutz of Scarsdale.

Many collections of works have contributed to this book, and I wish to thank the collectors who so thoughtfully permitted me to enter their homes or shops to photograph Louis Icart works in their possession. These persons include Phyllis Elliot of Oakenshield, New York City; Richard Golden and Gene Schmittle of the Golden Griffins, New Hope, Pennsylvania; Martin and Ladina Kwait, Philadelphia; Oswaldo Novaes of Joia, New York City; Robert and Ellyn Schoenberg, Westfield, New Jersey; Ken and Jean Smith of Smith's Art Shop, Roselle Park, New Jersey; Mrs. William Q. Tucker, West Hartford, Connecticut; Martin Wolpert and Michael Craven of Papillon in Los Angeles.

A very special thanks to Mel Karmel and to Audrey Miller for their vital help in organizing this volume and their fine friendship; to Reginald Wickman for important additional photography; and to Katharine M. McClinton for her excellent introduction. I also wish to thank Jane West, Elizabeth Congdon, Michael Fragnito, Ruth Smerechniak, and Janice Pargh of Clarkson N. Potter, Inc., for their valuable editorial advice.

Additionally I wish to thank Allan Kelley and Christina Mason for some critical translations and corrections; Nelson Kimmelman, Esq., for his important legal advice; Robert Rusting, for his patience; and Lila S. Garber, the important catalyst of it all.

I also wish to thank the staff of the Prints Division of the U.S. Library of Congress, and a special thanks to John Wayne of the U.S. Copyright Office.

Finally, I have three personal thank-you's—to my parents, who will now believe it; to Miriam Caplan, for her love and confidence; and to G.N.O.R., with all my love, for everything.

AUTHOR'S INTRODUCTION

36. But there are other creative sensibilities besides the seriousness (both tragic and comic) of high culture and of the high style of evaluating people. And one cheats oneself, as a human being, if one has respect only for the style of high culture, whatever else one may do or feel on the sly.

SUSAN SONTAG from
"Notes on 'Camp'" [1]

To FULLY COMPREHEND LOUIS ICART'S ROLE IN THE DEVELOPMENT OF THE POPULAR ARTS OF THE twentieth century, the serious student of Art Deco and its related arts must prepare for entry into the "yes but is it art?" controversy. For, in examining the works of Louis Icart we reach out for definitions such as indeed, is it art? And, if so, is it "serious" or "commercial"? Can the artist's work be classified as Art Deco? Or is it "camp"? Perhaps even "Kitsch"?

When the popularity of Icart's etchings was at its peak in France, as well as in the United States, in the late 1920s, the critics were divided like two opposing armies. Peyton Boswell, editor of the influential American periodical *Art Digest,* had little use for Louis Icart's etchings of languid French ladies. "It would be folly to urge any serious artist to paint (or etch) down to the doggerel level of the Icart formula," he wrote in a 1937 editorial. "To call such fine art is to strain the word's already sorely abused hospitality." [2]

Jules Lafforgue, a French art critic, took the opposite view, "His work is too 'pretty,' reproach his ignorant or jealous contemporaries. 'Pretty?' Certainly! And why cannot 'pretty' subjects be majestic as well? Must one today, to be considered a serious artist, paint ugly things? Or compose boring music? Surely Watteau, in the eyes of his contemporaries, was truly a 'serious' artist. Or was he less amusing, less 'pretty' than Louis Icart?" [3]

The controversy still lingers, fanned by the breezes of Icart's re-entry into the contemporary art scene. It is just this rebirth of interest in Icart's work, closely tied to the reappraisal of the decorative arts of the 1920s and 1930s, the Art Deco period, that has lifted this artist into a new realm of popularity.

One may hesitate to relate Icart directly to the Art Deco movement. Katharine Morrison McClinton, however, the first biographer of the period to recognize Icart as part of the Art Deco movement, is not reluctant to include him in her general survey, *Art Deco: A Guide for Collectors*.[4] She divides Art Deco into two distinct styles: first, the functional, geometric, machine-inspired styles typified by the agile geometry of the Chrysler Building in New York or the poster art of E. McKnight Kauffer and A. M. Cassandre; second, those styles dependent on feminine grace, smooth-flowing expression, and speed for their sources. The fashion drawings of Erté, many of the flowing crystal designs of René Lalique, or the porcelain female figures of the German *Volkstedt* factories may certainly be classed in this latter framework. Viewed from this perspective, the etchings of Louis Icart do indeed bear many of these features. Icart's etchings are rich in movement and grace, features they owe to the fine curvilinear lines of a steady etcher's hand. This aspect alone offers them entry into the world of Art Deco.

Icart's works, however, show other features that urge one to relate them to the arts of the period. The carefree effervescence of Icart's heroines is often reminiscent of every "roaring twenties" image—the champagne bubbles, the flapper, the Charleston, the speakeasy. Their fashions, certainly because they were created during that mad period, are typical of the times; furs, feather boas, and other accouterments of Jazz Age feminine charm are seen often in Icart's works.

Icart etchings, by their very nature as French exports, are identified with other Art Deco objects. Art Deco did, after all, take its name from the Exposition Internationale des Arts Décoratifs et Industriels Modernes, the 1925 Paris exposition that presented the fine and applied arts of the period as a unified entity. The magic words "imported from France" have been known to work miracles for many less artistic objects. The allure of the French identity of many Art Deco items is an important consideration when examining the American popular tastes of the 1920s and 1930s. In many ways, Icart's etchings are the epitome of French "chic," a quality with which many Americans chose to identify.

But while Icart's capricious ladies so typify the spirit of Art Deco, they are also the great-granddaughters of eighteenth-century ancestors. In several ways, Icart's works parallel the paintings of Jean Antoine Watteau (1684–1721), François Boucher (1703–70), and Jean Honoré Fragonard (1732–1806).

For example, the hedonistic nymph in Icart's *Dans les Branches* (The Swing), 1928 (Fig. 1), and the coy innocent in Fragonard's *L'Escarpolette* (The Swing), 1766 (Fig. 3), share many similarities. While there is no single work that embodies all the characteristics that make Icart's etchings so appealing, *Dans les Branches* conveys his sense of motion, coloring, composition, and the all-important touch of eroticism. Etched in 1928, this lady in midair is an updated version of Fragonard's subject. Fragonard's lady is a joyous symbol of springtime. Perhaps her exuberant swinging has surprised the shoe off her foot, and despite her whimsy, she is aware that her nearby suitor has an unrestricted view under her petticoats. Set against a backdrop of autumn leaves, Icart's vivacious miss has also lost her shoe, but her kick is as deliberate and calculated as is her recklessly exposed garter. Like her ancestor, she is bent on seduction, but her suitor is the viewer, who, seeing her reach the ultimate ascent of the swing, waits expectantly for her return.

Fig. 3. *L'Escarpolette* (The Swing) by Fragonard, oil, 1766, 32 x 35. (Courtesy of the Wallace Collection, London)

Both subjects typify the carefree *le joli* (the "good life") of the aristocracy. In the rococo canvases of the 1700s this was one of the few preferred topics for painting. King Louis XIV, who reigned from 1643 to 1715, and King Louis XV, who reigned from 1715 to 1774, greatly influenced the arts, and artists had to achieve royal acceptance before public acceptance of their works was possible. The eighteenth century was a time of peace and prosperity, a time in which the French aristocracy practiced social graces, a time when informal gatherings at the gardens of Versailles provided the elegant and leisurely backdrops so well suited to the tastes of the kings. Rome's influence on the arts of the day was also evident. Classical artifacts abound in the gardens and byways pictured by the artists of the day. In the *fêtes galantes* of Watteau, for example, one easily finds elements of the classic pastorale and of the theatricality of the *commedia dell'arte.*

Many of these same elements are found in Louis Icart's etchings. *La Biche Apprivoisée,* known in this country as *The Four Dears,* 1929 (Fig. 4), shows three elegant ladies in a lush garden where large trees cast mysterious shadows. Etchings like *L'Après-midi d'un Faune* (Afternoon of a Faun), circa 1920 (Fig. 5), combine the fantasy creatures of the Italian comedy with all the suggestiveness of dimly lit passageways in eighteenth-century gardens.

Icart's most obvious debt is to the work of Fragonard. Icart's striking *Minauche,* 1923 (Fig. 6), appears to have been modeled after Fragonard's *Un Garçon Comme Pierrot* (A Boy as Pierrot), 1765 (Fig. 7). The expression and composition are similar, but Icart has embellished his work with the fine sensitive lines which are so much a characteristic of drypoint. The work is one of Icart's most pleasing portraits, a picture that represents his young daughter, Reine, at an early age.

Icart shared many of the same personal experiences with Fragonard. Both artists made customary visits to Italy to study the art masterpieces of that country. Both employed historical settings in their works as a means of emphasizing the grace of their subjects. Both were expert technicians whose works conveyed sensuality and tenderness without delving too deeply into excessive eroticism. And both worked with great speed, a fact that sometimes left a distinct residue of momentum in their respective works.

Fig. 5. *L'Apres-midi d'un Faune* (Afternoon of a Faun), drypoint and etching, circa 1920, 13½ x 10½.

Fig. 4. *La Biche Apprivoisée* (The Four Dears), drypoint and etching, 1929, 15 x 21.

While Fragonard's elegant canvases had a strong influence on Icart, the paintings of Boucher inspired other parallels, a fact that brings to mind one critic's comments: "...nothing but young women with rouged, simpering faces. Such art is the degradation of taste, color, character, composition, expressive drawing...." [5] A harsh criticism, to say the least, and one, in fact, that could have applied to either artist. The words were actually directed at the work of Boucher by Denis Diderot (1713–84), the French encyclopedist and philosopher. The analogy is clear; Icart's etchings have been declared trifling according to just such standards.

Boucher's *The Bath of Diana*, 1742 (Fig. 8), features a young woman who is the principal figure in many of his works. Icart also favored using the same model repeatedly, his beautiful wife, Fanny. The wooded setting and the casual poses of the women are typical of both Boucher and Icart. In *Intimité* or, as it is sometimes called, *The Green Screen*, 1928 (Fig. 9), Icart mirrors the compositional elements found in Boucher's work. In his clever use of props, such as screens or windows, Icart was able to suggest the atmosphere of a wooded setting while maintaining an interior scene. Both artists, in addition, turned to opera and theatre for subject matter, and Boucher's preponderance of semidraped female figures was no small influence on Icart. *Baigneuses*

Fig. 6. *Minauche,* drypoint and etching, 1923, 11 x 14.

Fig. 7. *Un Garçon Comme Pierrot* (A Boy as Pierrot) by Fragonard, oil, 1765, 23½ x 19½. (Courtesy of the Wallace Collection, London)

Fig. 8. *The Bath of Diana* by Boucher, oil, 1742. (Courtesy of the Louvre, Paris)

Fig. 9. *Intimité* (The Green Screen), drypoint and etching, 1928, 18 x 16.

(Bathers), 1931 (Fig. 10), is similar to many works of Boucher, who favored such varied groupings of female figures.

In Watteau, Icart found other elements that proved critical to his compositions on copperplate. The pose seen in Watteau's *Lady at Her Toilette*, (Fig. 11), is a familiar one to admirers of Icart's works. The look of surprise, the luxurious bedchamber, the animated expressions of the dog and the statue to the lady's right remind us of elements seen in many Icart etchings. *L'Essayage* (The Pink Slip), 1939 (Fig. 12), shares many of these features.

Watteau was known for his placement of figures in his canvases. He broke away from the carefully balanced compositions of the Italians, constructing his pictures from figures that he had sketched from life on earlier occasions. Subject matter was less important than placement to Watteau, a characteristic element of many Icart etchings. In *Le Poème*, 1928 (Fig. 13), Icart has placed all the figures in distinct poses that seem to bear no relation to each other. Many of these same figures can be found again in other Icart works. The pose he gave the figure at the far right, for example, is seen again, in modified form, in *Danseuse*, 1931 (Fig. 14), as well as in the *In Homage to Beethoven*, an oil painting he executed in 1945 (Fig. 15).

Sketching his models from life before applying the designs to the copperplate, as Watteau did before painting, Icart provided many of his figures with studied, though natural-looking, attitudes. Like Watteau, Icart also posed his ladies with characters from mythology, Italian comedy, or literature.

In addition to Watteau, Boucher, and Fragonard, other French painters who stressed the "good life" in their works influenced Icart. Among them are Nicholas Lancret (1690–1743) and Jean-Baptiste Pater (1605–1736).

Icart's oil paintings were influenced by other artists. In the work of the Venetian painter Paolo Veronese (1528–88), Icart found heavy emphasis on decoration, splendid settings, and figures in richly decorated costumes. Many of his early oils exhibit the same characteristics. His misty landscapes of Italian cities, which he painted in the 1920s, owe a great debt to Francesco Guardi (1712-93). They are subtle, with monochromatic lighting that stresses mood rather than reality. This same feeling is seen in the work of Eugène Carrière (1849-1906), a French artist best known for his portraits of esteemed writers and artists such as Auguste Rodin, Anatole France, and Paul Verlaine. *Maternité*, 1893 (Fig. 16), has been called Carrière's greatest work, and Albert Besnard, a member of the Société des Artistes Français and a prominent engraver, once stated, "One day we will speak of Carrière's *Maternité* as we now speak of Michaelangelo's *Pièta*. [6] Besnard's miscalculation aside, the work's effect on Icart is clear. In the subtle tones of this painting, which depicted members of Carrière's family, Icart found the basis for a series of oils that would come to be known as *"les visions blanches,"* which contain the same mistiness of *Maternité*. Icart's own version of *Maternité* painted in the early 1930s (Fig. 17), forgoes sharp chiaroscuro in favor of delicate white and gray tones and soft modeling. The subtlety of the work is further enhanced by the image of the third child shrouded in a pearly haze in the left portion of the painting.

In his paintings, unlike his etchings, Icart emulates the French Impressionists, Claude Monet (1840-1926) and Edgar Degas (1834-1917). Icart openly spoke of himself as an "Impressionist" painter, and such *Visions Blanches* works as *Jeune Mère*, circa 1935 (Fig. 18), and *En Pensant à Watteau*, 1945 (Fig. 19), owe an obvious stylistic debt to Monet, Degas, and other Impressionist masters. Images of Degas's pastels of the dance are readily brought to mind on seeing Icart's *La Répétition*, 1940 (Fig. 21), a work that employs dramatic side lighting, to provide the effect of stage lights.

While the eighteenth-century artists and the Impressionists greatly influenced Icart, the popular artists of his own time also helped to mold him. In the pages of *Le Rire* and *Fantasio*, the important French periodicals of World War I and earlier, a young Icart first found the ideas for his future works. The humorous magazines featured amusing portraits of actresses and dancers, usually in exotic costumes and in poses to which Icart's memory would refer when he created many of his etchings. For example, an early issue of *Fantasio* displayed a series of photographs of a seminude anonymous dancer whose body was draped with a live boa constrictor. In 1934 Icart resurrected that image to provide the substance for *Grande Eve* (Eve and the Serpent; Fig. 20), a highly erotic, beautiful work that is one of Icart's greatest accomplishments.

Icart himself, in 1916, began providing illustrations for *Le Rire, Fantasio,* and *La Baïonette*. His cartoons were in the manner of Maurice Millière and Fabien Fabiano, contemporaries who were known for satiric drawings that featured beautiful women in various stages of dress and undress.

The "Great War," and, in turn, the rich patriotism that is so much a part of the French heritage, gave Icart enough artistic ammunition to create his compelling etchings of the period. In some cases, Icart borrowed directly from other artists. One striking example is *Le Baiser de Jeanne d'Arc* (The Kiss of Joan of Arc), an illustration by Louis Morin which appeared in a 1914 issue of *La Vie Parisienne,* the most famous of the early French humor magazines. The picture shows a stiff, winged Joan of Arc, in full armor, kissing a dying soldier. Icart later transformed this awkward bit of sentimentality into a graceful, eloquent etching, *Le Baiser de la Mère-Patrie* (The Kiss of the Motherland), 1918 (Fig. 22). The flowing garments of the beautiful angel who has come to kiss the dying Frenchman at the moment of death are in blue and red, while her bare torso is left white, hence the three colors of the French flag. The etching is a serious statement by an artist who had a personal reason for creating it: Icart's brother,

Fig. 11. *Lady at Her Toilette* by Watteau, oil, 1719.

Fig. 12. *L'Essayage* (The Pink Slip), drypoint and etching, 1939, 11 x 19.

Fig. 10. *Baigneuses* (Bathers), drypoint and etching, 1931, 17 x 24½.

Fig. 13. *Le Poème,* drypoint and etching, 1928, 22 x 18.

Fig. 14. *Danseuse,* drypoint and etching, 1931, 15 x 18½.

Fig. 15. *In Homage to Beethoven,* oil, 1945, 51 x 38.

Raymond, was killed in action during the war. The etching, which Icart dedicated to his mother, was in memory of her fallen son. This important early work clearly displays Icart's characteristic use of fine lines and his deft handling of engraving tools.

Icart developed his techniques as an etcher by studying the works of certain contemporaries, most notably Manuel Robbe (1872–1943) and Paul-César Helleu (1859–1927). Both these men gained fame for their fine etchings of women of high fashion. Robbe's works were finely detailed studies of ladies placed in interiors typical of the period. Helleu, on the other hand, was primarily a portrait artist, who emphasized expression and facial characteristics by deft use of the engraving needle.

Their Parisiennes of the turn of the century were modernized by Icart into magnificent specimens of French beauty that thrilled hearts on two continents. They gleefully rejuvenated spirits in times that were tired of respective bouts with warfare, recession, and national malaise.

The women of Louis Icart are the women of France as we have imagined them to be and as the French hope they will remain forever. Icart's mademoiselle knows the Elysian delight of Eve taking her first eager bite of the apple. She has the grace and mocking innocence of Manon Lescaut. She is Leda, Venus, Scheherazade, and Joan of Arc, all wrapped up into an irresistible package. Her admirers span continents and decades, and her power over us is as strong today as it was a generation ago, thanks to the artist's timeless portrayal of her beauty.

Small wonder that the United States of the 1920s and 1930s was fertile ground for the sale of Icart's ebullient works. Not only did the etchings give the consumer an opportunity to identify with French "chic," but in many ways, they possessed the same charisma as movies, which had impregnated themselves deeply into the American way of life. Icart's etchings were glamorous, carefree, and, best of all, relatively inexpen-

Fig. 16. *Maternité* by Carrière, oil, 1893. (Courtesy of the Louvre, Paris)

Fig. 17. *Maternité*, oil, circa 1930, 31½ x 25½.

Fig. 19. *En Pensant à Watteau* (Thinking of Watteau), oil, 1945, 17¾ x 20¼.

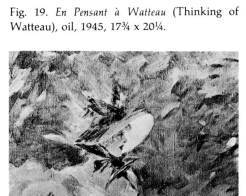

Fig. 18. *Jeune Mère* (Young Mother), oil, circa 1935.

Fig. 20. *Grand Eve* (Eve and the Serpent), drypoint and etching, 1934, 20 x 30.

Fig. 21. *La Répétition,* oil, 1940, 28 x 23.

sive. For between ten and forty dollars, an American family could decorate its living room or bedroom wall with a Paris "original."

As the country braced itself for the Second World War, American tastes drifted away from the elegant frivolities of Icart etchings, and by the time the war ended in 1945, Icart was virtually forgotten. Nearly thirty years passed before the serendipitous rediscovery of his works. They have entered the public eye on the same vehicle as the nostalgic interest in the 1920s, a growing appreciation of Art Deco, and a broader awareness of "camp."

It is this last term that presents the greatest problem in studying the works of Louis Icart, since it is a term that has been applied frequently to his etchings. Some people have even viewed them as "Kitsch," that element of "camp" that steps beyond its initial boundaries into the world of bad taste.

In her penetrating essay, "Notes on 'Camp,' " which was quoted at the outset, Susan Sontag, critic and filmmaker, attempts to pinpoint the exact meaning of "camp" taste. In a list of "camp" items, Ms. Sontag includes such obvious candidates as the films of Busby Berkeley, the Brown Derby restaurant on Sunset Boulevard in Los Angeles, and women's clothes of the 1920s. Yet "Notes on 'Camp' " was written in

1964, a year in which her list of "camp" items could still include, without much contention, the lamps of Louis C. Tiffany, Aubrey Beardsley drawings, and Lynd Ward's novel in woodcuts, *God's Man*. One need only look at recent writings about, and the exhibits of, the Art Nouveau period to hesitate before classifying Tiffany and Beardsley as "camp." The financial worth of Tiffany lamps and Beardsley drawings today would seem to lift them out of the "camp" category. And certainly the powerful works of Lynd Ward—especially *God's Man*—are today accepted as important milestones in the history of twentieth-century American book illustration. "Camp" taste therefore is highly dependent on current fashions, on the perspective in which the objects so deemed are viewed. If Icart's etchings are "camp" now, a reappraisal of his talent, as well as a move farther away from his contemporary scene, may well change that opinion. Today's collector's market, which has already seen the price of some Icart etchings rise into the thousands of dollars, has encouraged a new examination of his work that may, in the future, remove the name of Icart from the limitations of "camp."

Quite simply, Icart was an *artist*, in every sense of the word. His skill as an etcher was unmatched by any of his contemporaries, such as Maurice Millière, Valla Mora, and other artists who supplied etchings for the decorative picture trade. Trained observers will find a complex mixture of graphic arts techniques in many of Icart's works; drypoint, aquatint, *manière noire*, sugar lift, and dozens of other printmaking techniques were at his disposal, and at various times, in various ways, the artist found a use for them all.

Icart's reputation as an artist, however, does not rest on the merits of his etchings alone. In style, his oil paintings range from the *manière rouge* works of the early 1920s, paintings in which tones of red and gold predominated, to the Impressionistic series, *"les visions blanches,"* of the 1930s and '40s. His ability to convey sensuality and humor, characteristics so evident in his etchings, achieved an even finer focus in his oil paintings, and often he painted subjects of a more solemn nature. In a series of gripping canvases called *L'Exode* (The Exodus), Icart recorded the brutalization of his countrymen during World War II, bringing all the terrors of the German invasion of France back to mind with blunt accuracy.

In addition, as a creator of illustrations for nearly twenty limited edition books, Icart explored the various graphic arts in depth. His illustrations reveal another side of the artist, one which could inextricably blend his illustrations with their accompanying prose and poetry. Icart's love of literature led him to fertile fields for illustration, and his understanding and sensitivity toward the works he illustrated resulted in masterpieces of book illustration.

Icart's friendships with the modern poet Audiberti, as well as with authors Paul Yaki and Gabrielle Colette, brought him into close touch with the thinking of France's important writers. His own literary creations—*Don Quichotte de la Mancha* and *Rabelais*, two verse plays in the style of Edmond Rostand—reveal him to have a thorough understanding of the poetic process.

During his career, Icart supplemented his talents as an artist and poet with fashion designing, acting, flying, and gourmet cooking. His considerable financial success, primarily due to the etchings which he exported to the United States, allowed him to explore all these areas of interest, some to fruition, others not.

This volume reintroduces Louis Icart to the American public, who are now perhaps prepared to view his work objectively. The artist's work, having brought honor and respect from admiring French contemporaries, is presented in the hope of deriving the same appreciation from modern viewers.

Fig. 22. *Le Baiser de la Mère-Patrie* (The Kiss of the Motherland), drypoint and etching, 1918, 11½ x 19, edition of 100.

CHAPTER 1

Fig. 23. Icart at seven years as Luis in *Lorenzaccio*.

A
GOLDEN
LIFE

THE FIRST SON OF JEAN AND ELISABETH ICART WAS OFFICIALLY NAMED LOUIS JUSTIN LAURENT Icart, but the initials L.I. would be sufficient in this household. So from the moment of his birth, in the early morning hours of September 12, 1888, he was dubbed "Helli" (pronounced *el-ē*).

Helli was a rambunctious, vocal infant, and Jean Icart hoped that such vitality would last throughout his lifetime to equip him well for the difficult worlds of business or banking. A banker himself, he envisioned his new son in the same career. Jean was a tall, impressive-looking man of fair complexion. While his goatee and mustache were prominent features, his scalp had already begun to peer through a thinning cover of light brown hair. His son, however, resembled his wife's side of the family. Dark and round, he already had the same expressive black eyes—and certainly Helli would never be plagued by loss of hair.

Elisabeth Girot Icart stood a full foot beneath her husband in height, and what she lacked in stature, she made up for in girth. Helli was destined to take after the Girot side of the family, without a doubt.

The Icart family lived modestly in a small brick home on rue Traversière-de-labalance, in the southern French city of Toulouse. It was a quiet, sunny city, and untroubled by the growing pains typical of such cities as Marseille. Despite the developing industries and the busy Garonne River which bordered the city, Toulouse was still conservative. It was an old city, one in which respect for the arts was strong. A center of medieval culture, Toulouse was rich in Gothic architecture. *Académie des Jeux Floraux*, the famous annual poetry competitions which began in the year 1223, were still an important annual event. The city was also the home of many prominent writers and artists; the most famous, of course, was Henri de Toulouse-Lautrec, the artist and poster maker.

In this cultural atmosphere Helli was rapidly introduced to the pleasures of the fine arts. In 1894 Helli was enrolled in L'Ecole Chrétienne des Frères, a Catholic primary school near the Icart home. From the beginning Helli brought his parents exemplary school grades. Yet Jean Icart was far from content. His son's mathematical studies still needed improvement, and he demanded increased vigor in such studies. What, after all, was a banker without sound knowledge of figures and mathematical concepts? But at such an early age, Helli showed little interest in things that competed so rigorously with the joys of childhood.

By age seven, Helli had developed an outrageous talent for making people laugh, and he employed it frequently. He was popular with other students at l'Ecole, and he quickly found a place for himself among his young contemporaries.

Hoping to please his father, he applied himself diligently to the study tasks demanded of him. Eventually, Elisabeth Icart gave birth to another son, Raymond, and young Louis found the family's attentions diverted to the new arrival. It was not long before the young Icart developed other ambitions.

Free from parental disapproval, Louis was introduced to the theatre when he was selected to play small parts in school productions of such Romantic dramas as *Lorenzaccio*, by Alfred de Musset (1810-57), a French playwright who emulated the dramas of Victor Hugo (1802-85). The youngster appeared in elaborate costumes (Fig. 23), and this introduction to the magic of theatre had a profound effect on him. Helli dreamed of someday becoming an actor, of being the star performer at La Comédie Française. After appearing in various roles in school productions, he was selected for the most Romantic part he ever played, the title role in *Ruy Blas* (Fig. 24), Hugo's 1838 verse play about a Spanish servant who becomes Prime Minister of Spain, wins the love of the Queen, and institutes various social reforms. Helli was the obvious choice for the role among the other aspirants. By this time he had prematurely developed a deep, rich voice, and, for one so young, he did indeed have a fine comprehension of the meaning of Hugo's verse. The performance was a great success, the capstone of Helli's seven years at l'Ecole.

That fall Louis Icart entered l'Ecole supérieure de commerce de Toulouse at rue des Trente-six Ponts to continue his studies for a career in business or banking. But with the discovery of Hugo's works and the thrill of acting, those trades seemed now even less interesting. Helli borrowed whatever books he could find by Hugo in the library, devouring the tales that were rich in romantic imagery and the dilemmas of the human condition. Hugo's work abandoned all the rules of classical tragedy. His verse plays—*Cromwell* (1827), *Hernani* (1830), and his prose work, *Lucrèce Borgia* (1833)—dealt with elemental conflicts—good and evil, beauty and ugliness, happiness and sadness. Reading the author's complex novels, the young student began to comprehend the intricate network of French history, taking great pleasure in *Les Misérables* (1862) and *Notre-Dame de Paris* (1831).

Helli's interest in Victor Hugo led him into relationships with fellow students with

Fig. 24. Icart, at age 15, in the title role of Victor Hugo's *Ruy Blas,* in a grammar school production.

whom he could share these works. One such friend was Jules Esquirol, who likewise focused his ambitions on the French theatre. Together, they gave impromptu readings of Hugo's works in the Esquirol home which were received with great enthusiasm by their friends. The two actors would practice their dialogues for hours. As Esquirol later recalled, "In my room, with the windows open, we roared the Alexandrines of the great one. One angry tenant called out, 'My God, there are madmen in the house.' But we continued anyway, knowing that the performers of the Théâtre Français would pale before us." [7]

Through his love of the theatre young Louis developed a taste for all the arts. Toulouse was a city rich in history and culture whose several art museums and galleries offered him his first introduction to the visual and performing arts.

These early visits to museums and galleries in his city prompted an eager Icart—at that time anxious to try his hand at all forms of creativity—to sketch small pictures as gifts for his family members. Most were awkward, unpromising landscapes or seascapes, but they were not unappreciated. On Helli's fourteenth birthday, he received a box of oil paints from his grandfather, a gift the young student relished far more than the very practical watch given him by his father.

But the urge to paint, though it offered a pleasant diversion, was not as strong as his urge to act. He became manipulative to achieve these ends, as illustrated by the following anecdote: In a lengthy essay on their lifelong friendship, Jules Esquirol recalled Icart's new patent leather shoes with buttons, a somewhat dubious gift from his mother. The shoes were in the window of a shop on the rue Alsace-Lorraine in downtown Toulouse. They cost fourteen francs, a sum that outraged Madame Icart, but Helli had said he wanted them desperately, and they were, after all, from one of the finest stores in the city. After much pleading, Elisabeth gave her son the money for the shoes. The next day Helli bought the identical shoes for nine francs fifty centimes at a discount store called L'Incroyable. Then, Helli and Jules, delighting in such cleverness, made plans to meet at Soubirous, a fine bookstore on rue Lafayette, to buy *Les Burgraves,* a handsomely illustrated volume of Victor Hugo's last play (1841) that the two future actors had admired daily in the front window of the store as they passed on their way to school. A rendezvous was arranged and Jules arrived at the appointed time. Icart, however, never appeared. Jules waited until the shop closed, with still no word from his fellow Hugophile. The next day a sullen and embarrassed Louis Icart appeared at the school.

"Oh what a scene there was at my home last evening," he confessed. "I had taken off my new shoes and put them at the foot of the bed. I went downstairs to wash up when I heard a terrible commotion. I went up and saw my mother shaking the shoes at me and calling me a 'miserable black sheep.' She had seen the name l'Incroyable inscribed on the sole, and everyone knows the price of shoes there. I had to give back the rest of the money. She hit me two times and sent me to bed without my supper." [8]

Louis Icart was never able to purchase *Les Burgraves,* but the beauty of this illustrated book may have planted an early seed that would eventually blossom into his own activity as an illustrator of fine books.

The young student's love for the theatre continued, however, in spite of the incident with the shoes. At the Théâtre des Variétés, Icart and Esquirol attended, among other French dramas and operettas, productions of Hugo's *Lucrèce Borgia* and *Sevéro Torelli* by François Coppée. They would return from each performance reciting the passages they knew by heart.

"At that time," his friend reflected later, "one would never think that Icart would become the painter and etcher that we know today. He was not a genius in his art classes, and the subjects he produced in conté crayon were undistinguished. His creations were merely in proportion." [9]

Indeed, Helli had no idea that he would someday find his place in the world as an artist, and he directed all his energies to the theatre. However, by the time he was sixteen, Icart stood only five feet tall, hardly a height suited to the romantic leading roles in which he had imagined himself. Fortunately, his continued eager participation in school dramatic productions gave him a taste of other aspects of the theatre such as set and costume design. He even tried writing verse plays of his own, but these were uncompleted efforts never publicly presented. Helli was determined to develop various theatrical abilities, certain that one day one of them would open the door to an acting career.

Ironically, in later years, it was the secondary goals that Icart accomplished on a professional basis: designing sets and costumes for the Paris Opera, and writing his own verse plays, *Don Quichotte de la Manche* and *Rabelais.* Only acting, his first and greatest love, would be denied him.

During his last year at the business school, Helli told his father of his ambitions. He did not want to be a businessman or a banker, but an actor, and he asked his father to pay his way through acting school. The answer was a firm no; his father contended there was no security in an actor's life and no future, especially for a lad of such small stature. Helli would have to pursue an acting career on his own.

Louis expected the reaction, but at least his father had not insisted that he take a position with a bank. He would work for a period of time in Toulouse, and, when he had saved enough money, he would leave for Paris where his career as an actor would begin.

At age sixteen, Helli and Jules, diplomas in hand, approached a Toulouse job agency for work. Jules obtained a clerical post at a local distillery which brought him the handsome sum of forty francs per month. Icart took a job at a smaller salary with an architect's office. The work involved routine copying of diagrams, and Helli often used his free time to draw cartoons and sketches—while dreaming of ways to make his entry into the Paris theatre world.

A military obligation came first, however, and after only a few months with the architect, Icart was drafted into the French infantry. Because of his eagerness to achieve his professional ambitions, Icart's experience with the military was unpleasant and unsatisfying, and he anxiously awaited his return to civilian life.

Jules Esquirol had also been drafted into the army, although he was stationed with the commissary. The two friends maintained their contact during their army years, sustaining one another's dreams of the theatre. A few months after being discharged, the two novice performers descended on Paris with a vigor and enthusiasm matched only by their naïveté.

While awaiting the "right" employment in Paris, Icart earned money in various odd jobs, among them walking the streets as a "sandwich," between two boards which advertised a restaurant. After several weeks, during which his limited sum of money was practically exhausted, Icart found a position with a small studio that designed and distributed postcards. His task was to hand-color the works of other artists.

Like dozens of small postcard manufacturers in the city that were modeled after Noyer, a major producer of postcards, Icart's employer created photographic and artist-drawn images of female models, known as "actresses," for export out of France. France was the birthplace of the artist's postcard, a highly salable little item inspired by the posters of Jules Chéret (1836–1932), Pierre Bonnard (1867–1947), and Théophile-Alexandre Steinlen (1859–1923), whose images of graceful ladies had become ever-present in Paris. And too, the naughty mademoiselles who appeared in the popular magazine *La Vie Parisienne* had a great influence on the postcards that were designed for export.

Icart's functions at the postcard company were critical to his development as an artist. There he was exposed to the subject that would eventually become his trademark—the slightly risqué Parisienne—and there he learned the various graphic arts techniques employed in making 5 ½" × 3 ½" pictures. Etching and aquatint were most commonly employed, but lithograph and photoreproduction processes were used for certain types of cards. Icart's experience at the firm provided him with training that might have taken years to learn at an art school. Within a few months, Icart was creating postcard designs of his own, and in 1907 and 1908, he created hundreds of pictures, still using "Helli" as his signature.

Icart and Esquirol, the latter having obtained a post with an insurance company, attended whatever theatrical events they could afford. At the Folies Bergère and other cabaret entertainments, Icart was fascinated by the lavish costumes and settings, and in his spare time at the postcard studio, he sketched fantastic costume designs of his own. The two friends still amused their acquaintances with exuberant recitations of Hugo's verse, but the bent of Icart's soul had already begun to take a different direction.

His first apartment was in a furnished hotel on rue des Batignolles, equidistant from the artists' quarter of Montmartre and the fashionable area near l'Arc de Triomphe. Icart often spent Sundays strolling down the Champs-Elysées or visiting the Louvre Museum. Before drinking in the glories of the European masters, however, he would take in the visual delights of *les femmes chics,* those elegant examples of Parisian high society at its grandest. Heralding the beauty of Paris in their Sunday dress, these demoiselles, escorted by family or gentlemen friends, or occasionally in pairs, floated gracefully along the boulevard or sat for hours in the colorful sidewalk cafés.

Paris offered still other images that impressed the neophyte artist/actor. Advertising posters decorated Paris and most certainly were noticed and admired by Icart. Works by Jules Chéret, who created over a thousand posters during his lifetime, did not escape Icart's eye. Chéret's graceful female figures, often depicted in frenzied motion, earned him the name "Steam Watteau," and the same exciting sense of motion would eventually appear in many of the etchings of Louis Icart.

It was in the Louvre Museum, however, that Icart found his greatest inspiration. The canvases of eighteenth-century French masters were as rich a treasure as he would

Fig. 25. *Les Hortensias* (Hydrangeas), drypoint and etching, 1929, 21 x 17.

find anywhere. And other artistic voices—those of Monet, Renoir, Degas, and the other Impressionist painters—would find their way into Icart's work.

The young artist attended every exhibition of the Paris Salon which was sponsored by the Société des Artistes Français. Its tastes were determined by the influential Ecole des Beaux-Arts, a rather rigid institution that had not divested itself of the classical tastes that were designed for earlier generations of art patrons. Icart also attended the exhibitions of the Salon des Indépendants, Salon de la Jeune Peinture, Salon de Mai, and the Salon des Réalités Nouvelles. In each exhibition, the artists represented some form of breaking away from the established, obligatory *beaux-arts* tastes.

Another feature of the Paris cityscape was to have a lasting impression on Icart. A unique biweekly magazine was begun in August 1906, and Icart was ripe to embrace its philosophies and pleasures. *Fantasio, magazine gai,* was to have the strongest influence on Icart's later work, providing him with a series of images that would express themselves in later years. Based loosely on the American magazine *Life* and England's *Punch, Fantasio* was filled with brief, though often irreverent, commentaries on everyday life in France. Few subjects escaped satirization, and Icart especially relished the erotic undertones of a magazine that would never have been permitted in the home of Jean Icart.

An early issue of *Fantasio* featured an article on Fragonard, "Le Peintre des galanteries," an item that Icart no doubt considered carefully. Often the magazine featured full-page photographs or paintings of prominent persons, sometimes actresses or dancers. *La femme aux hortensias,* a painting by Laissement, contained a soft-focus impression of a woman in a large picture hat, seated among hydrangea plants. It was the obvious inspiration for *Les Hortensias* (Fig. 25), a 1929 work that became the most popular etching Icart ever created. Icart's early sketchbooks, which he quickly filled during his first years in Paris, show copies of works that appeared in *Fantasio* and other early humor magazines.

Icart did not forget the theatre; indeed, he still participated in private readings of Hugo's verse with his friend Esquirol, but while praises were sung for both actor and artist, it was Icart the artist who began to obscure Icart the actor.

Using pastel crayons, Icart once designed the program for a four-part play written by Esquirol and presented at an informal gathering in the home of an acquaintance. The drawing featured a melancholy blonde seated in a dimly lit garden, while the lights of a party blazed in a house behind her. When Esquirol praised the drawing, Icart said, "There are times when I amuse myself this way. It is curious. One could say a mysterious force controls my pencil. I can't explain it." [10]

After purchasing the essentials—food, wine, and clothing—Icart's remaining francs went for the basic supplies of a painter. He had found joy in the creation of beauty on paper, and he seems, at this point to have found his calling as an artist.

Icart was anxious to share his new "success" with his father, and he soon sent him a photograph of himself in the studio at work on a new canvas (Fig. 26). Louis wrote under the picture, "For my father, the corner of my studio where I think well of him."

Icart's decision to become an artist did not restrict him to oil painting. Through acquaintances the young artist developed at social gatherings and drama readings, he met Léon Pavi, editor of *La Critique Théâtrale,* a monthly magazine devoted to criticism and behind-the-scenes glimpses of Paris theatre. Icart was invited to design covers for his periodical. In December 1908, the words *dessin d'Helli* appeared for the first time on the cover of a magazine. Thereafter, Icart became a regular contributor to the same publication. Most of his drawings were of spindly-legged characters who were appearing in current Paris productions (detail, Fig. 27), but these were atypical of Icart. It was the female form that captivated him and the desire to clothe it in the trappings of his fancy.

Fig. 26. The young artist in his first Paris studio. The inscription reads, "To my dear father, this corner of my studio where I think well of him."

Fig. 27. Detail from Icart's first cover for *La Critique Théâtrale.*

The transition from postcards to magazine covers to fashion design was not an easy one. While catalogs of his etchings, later to be published in the United States by the Louis Icart Society, were rich with glamorous tales of his instant success at the tender age of sixteen, Icart was in reality faced with the double handicap of no formal training and little money. In fact, the early Paris years were often times of lean poverty. Once, during these destitute times, Icart, with great remorse, stole some potatoes from an outdoor market for his dinner. Many years later, to absolve himself the artist gave the merchant an original etching, inscribed, "In thanks for your three potatoes, Louis Icart." [11]

Poverty, however, was not Icart's destiny. Industrious and determined, he sought work with the couturiers; he took his postcard designs, drawings, and other spare-time works to the major fashion studios of Paris. His first commission came from la Maison Valmont, a designer of hats and accessories on rue Royale. Though usually nude, Icart's postcard ladies sometimes wore headgear, generally outlandish creations of birds, feathers, fruits, and other assorted flora and fauna. Maison Valmont was more interested in Icart's hat designs than his naked ladies, and he was put to work interpreting the ideas of other designers for catalogs and other printed media. While Icart did find the opportunity to design a few hats of his own, he felt more comfortable with other areas of the *toilette,* and he quickly learned the basics of designing gowns, dresses, and miscellaneous essentials of the feminine wardrobe. He submitted his designs to other Paris fashion studios, and within a few months he added to his commissions with activities for Paquin, Redfern, Premet, Worth, Bechoff-David, Jenny, Beer, and Patou. Icart's drawings for these studios began to appear in the major fashion publications of the day: *Gazette du Bon Ton, Luxe de Paris, Femina,* and *Jardin de la Mode,* among others. Unfortunately the artist had not yet achieved a significant reputation and most of his drawings for such publications were merely marginal decorations or unsigned sketches.

Illustrating for these publications, Icart occasionally employed the *pochoir* process, which uses stencils to achieve a rich, colorful thickness of paint. A 1914 issue of *Luxe de Paris* features just such a creation, done for the studio of Bechoff-David (Fig. 28). The scene is typical of Icart's early fashion illustration and it shows great similarities to Icart's etching *Le Chaperon Rouge* (Red Riding Hood), 1927 (Fig. 29).

Fig. 28. *Pochoir* illustration for Bechoff-David studio, 1914.

Fig. 29. *Le Chaperon Rouge* (Red Riding Hood), dry-point, 1927, 14 x 21.

At the time that Icart worked for these major design studios, fashions were undergoing major transition, from the nineteenth to the twentieth century. Women were eager to divest themselves of the heavy overflow of lace, cotton, buckles, and high necklines worn by their mothers. New trends called for higher waistlines, a return to Empire styling, and clothing that clung to the body rather than billowing out. The designs of the great couturier Paul Poiret, the major influence behind this trend, were known throughout the world; the new look was so appealing that most fashion houses adapted it according to their own tastes. An Icart fashion illustration from *Luxe de Paris* (Fig. 30)—this one for the Premet studio—is typical of the then-current fashion vogue in Paris.

Fig. 30. Original *pochoir* by Icart for the fashion magazine *Luxe de Paris,* 1914.

During these early years, prior to the First World War, Icart established a pattern of working that would remain with him throughout his busy career. "I work on those days that God himself chose to work," he said once, "and at the rate of eight to ten hours of labor a day, a man can accomplish much in a year." [12] Rising at six each morning, Icart would linger for an hour over *croissants* and coffee, then work without interruption until early afternoon. He would stop for a two-hour luncheon and then work again until nightfall.

During this productive period, when assignments from fashion houses provided him with enough income to expand his studio, he continued his experiments in the graphic arts. He had found his subject—the beautiful women of Paris—and though he sketched them in fashions as part of his livelihood, he felt the urge to interpret them from an artist's standpoint. Icart began his work on copperplate during this period. While he could not afford an etching press of his own, he was able to use the facilities of various ateliers, which rented their equipment to artists by the hour. Working quickly and diligently, Icart had completed dozens of etchings by the end of 1911. The women he etched were the models he sketched at the fashion design studios, and the influence of that occupation was evident in his earlier work.

During his early career with the fashion houses, Icart met a young widow who was employed in the offices of one of the fashion studios. She was a few years older than Icart and had a small child. Icart, taken with the romance of Paris, and anxious to fill the lonely hours, proposed marriage. The couple was married in 1912 and Icart adopted the child. His decision was a hasty one, and within a few months Icart realized his unfortunate mistake. He distracted himself with his work.

The artist searched in vain for a Paris gallery that would offer him a one-man showing, now that he had a sufficient quantity of works to present. Finally, in July 1912, Icart's contacts at one of the fashion studios helped him to arrange a one-man exhibition at a gallery in Barcelona. The Spanish city was hardly the arts center he had hoped for, but the experience prepared him for future exhibits. In November of that year, two of the etchings that were displayed in Barcelona were seen in Paris at the Salon des Ironistes, an annual exhibit of the work of cartoonists and other humor artists. The exhibit was devoted to "the woman," and twenty-five artists displayed their work. While the critical response to the exhibit was generally favorable, one critic made specific mention of Icart, "Finally, there is Louis Icart, who has adapted the drypoint so well to the slim, supple form and elegance of the modern Parisienne." [13] *Fruit Défendu* (Forbidden Fruit), circa 1912 (Fig. 31), was one of the Icart works on display. It is a charming etching that was later marketed in the United States.

The year 1913 was a busy one for Louis Icart. His work for *La Critique Théâtrale* was brought to the attention of Maurice Neumont, famed poster artist and cartoonist, and a founder of the Société des Dessinateurs-humoristes, an organization of artists and illustrators who became very influential during the First World War. Neumont invited Icart to participate in the third annual exhibition of the Salon des Dessinateurs-humoristes, to be held in April of that year at the gallery La Boëtie. Icart's works were thus again seen in a Paris gallery, this time sharing wall space with such prestigious names as Jules Chéret, Adolphe Willette, Francisque Poulbot, Charles LaBorde, and Hermann-Paul.

His appearance in this group exhibit encouraged other galleries to take Icart's creations into their group presentations. In November of 1913, in an exhibit of *la gravure originale en couleur* at the influential Galerie Georges Petit, Icart presented his new etchings.

A year later, a one-man exhibit of his work was organized by the Paris fashion

Fig. 31. *Fruit Défendu* (Forbidden Fruit), drypoint and etching, circa 1912, 13 x 17½.

Fig. 32. *Le Golf*, 1913, drypoint and etching, 11 x 17. (Collection of the Library of Congress)

magazine *Gazette du Bon Ton* in Brussels at la Salle Aeolian. The proximity to Paris was encouraging, but the reviews were not.

Said the Brussels weekly *La Vie Intellectuelle*, "Monsieur Icart, who draws well enough, with a style of finesse and delicacy, has not sufficiently removed himself from the concerns of fashion design to give his works character and allure." [14] *Indépendance Belge*, a daily, was even less kind: "If he had shown only four works, instead of the forty presented, the effect would have been better, since, at present, the lack of diversity in this monotonous grouping convinces us of a lack of imagination and narrowness of vision." [15]

Le Golf (Fig. 32) is a 1913 work that is typical of the etchings seen in the exhibit. It features a young woman in a bright orange sweater swinging a golf club. The characteristic flair for motion and composition that Icart developed in later years is definitely missing in this etching.

The disappointing reviews in Brussels crushed Icart, who, at twenty-five, saw his dream of a one-man Paris exhibit disappearing from sight. Discouraged, but not defeated, he continued to work in copper and in oil paint in between his fashion sketching.

Early in 1914 Icart met a magical, effervescent eighteen-year-old named Fanny Volmers (Fig. 33) who was to change the course of his life. She was at this time an employee of the fashion house Paquin, assigned to search out commissions for new designs. The future husband and wife met by chance one morning when Icart arrived to show a new portfolio of drawings.

A petite Parisian blonde with inquisitive eyes and remarkably graceful hands, Fanny was, as Icart later said, "more than beautiful." [16] He could not resist her captivating appearance, and he asked her to pose for him. From the moment of their meeting, she captured his heart and became the inspiration for his work from then on.

Fig. 33. Fanny Volmers.

This winsome elf with penetrating eyes possessed an independent nature. She, too, was an artist—a painter and sculptress—but her abilities were limited and her success small. She was to achieve immortality of a different sort. Their love affair was to last for over thirty-five years. Her beauty was enough to transform any artist's canvas into an attractive picture and with Louis Icart as the painter, some works became masterpieces. His swift, flowing lines followed the shapely curves of her body, and her delicate hands became features of almost every new etching. But most important, the blossoming of this joyous relationship could be sensed in each new Icart creation.

Fanny was the daughter of Alfred Volmers, a Parisian cabinetmaker and his wife, Marie Celestine. Not the glamorous high-society *femme fatale* that Icart pictured in many early works, she dreamed of becoming a fashion model but was hindered in her career ambitions by her small and somewhat broad stature. A beautiful woman, nevertheless, she would eventually see her image immortalized in thousands of artworks by her suitor. When she met Louis Icart, Fanny knew very little of the French theatre and Victor Hugo. Her capacity to adapt, however, soon involved her in Louis's interests. The romance of Hugo's poetry and the exuberance of the eighteenth century were woven into their love affair and in the spring of 1914, Icart left his wife and the couple moved together into an apartment/artist's studio on rue Sainte-Anne.

It was one of the artist's best seasons. Not only was he living with the woman he worshiped, but his works were being exhibited in the galleries of Paris and selling well. Further recognition came on May 17, 1914, when the King and Queen of Denmark, who were in France on a state visit, attended a special performance at L'Elysée by members of the Paris Opera ballet corps, in their honor. While the newspaper reports neglected to mention the quality of the performances by a M Aveline and Mlle Zambelli, particular notice was taken of their costumes which were designed by Louis Icart.

Shortly thereafter, Icart received his first major award, the Diplôme d'Honneur, for etchings which he had exhibited at l'Exposition de Gand, an annual event in Belgium.

The first year of their affair was a year of ascension for both Louis and Fanny, and though they wanted to marry, Icart's wife, who was a practicing Catholic, would not grant him a divorce. The First World War reared its angry head in August 1914 and like most of the French, Louis and Fanny were not prepared for a long war. The beginning of World War I was viewed almost as an exciting diversion by many citizens who expected it to end within a few weeks. Little did they expect bloody trench warfare that would last four years and bring death to over one million people. But by November 1914, Icart had realized its impact and was drafted into the infantry.

This time, however, his reputation as an artist allowed him to select the part he would play in the struggle against *les boches*. Assigned to the 131st battalion, Icart was stationed near the French village of Mailly. While the first several months were spent strictly as a *poilu*, Icart was later assigned to the *bureau de dessin* where he learned to interpret aerial photographs for later transfer to maps and charts. While the rudiments of mapmaking were of foremost importance to Icart, he found time to use the artist's materials which were at his disposal for more satisfying purposes, such as drawing sketches and cartoons that delighted his fellow soldiers.

While Icart made the most of his time in the service, he was deeply saddened by his separation from Fanny. She wrote to him daily, long lonely letters that he answered with poems, sketches, and passionate monologues. In many ways their letters were like those of Victor Hugo and his mistress Juliette Drouet, the actress who left her career to become his lover. During Hugo's exile from France for over twenty years, he shared over fifteen thousand letters with his absent lover. While Louis and Fanny were perhaps not so intense, or verbose, their love was no less passionate than that of any other famous duet having suffered the agonies of separation.

Both lovers waited anxiously for Icart's periodic, though infrequent, leaves, when he would rush to Paris by any means possible to be with Fanny, if only for a few hours. In August 1915, Icart was granted leave to return to Paris for a special occasion—Fanny had given birth to their first and only child, a girl, and they named her Reine, meaning queen.

Fanny and her baby lived in the apartment and studio that Icart had rented on rue Sainte-Anne. She had given up her post at Paquin and could now devote more time to acting as Icart's agent while he was at the front. The etchings he had printed before the war provided a healthy source of income during this period. Fanny diligently approached every gallery and art shop she thought would be interested in handling her lover's works. She worked with a vigor that would certainly have matched his own had he been able to solicit the galleries himself.

For Icart, the time spent at the front was not a complete waste. He was a regular contributor to *L'Echo des gourbis* (The Echo of the Shacks, in reference to the ramshackle buildings that made up the camp near Mailly), a small magazine that served as the combined expression of the men who made up the 131st *territoriale*. The publication was printed near the base in the village of Châlons-sur-Marne, and it was modeled after similar publications produced by the French Army. The small magazine appeared irregularly, only when there was enough time and energy left in the men to take on a new edition. The tiny morale booster was then distributed to other battalions and to sources in Paris, by which the magazine was presented to civilian audiences.

In a preface to *Tous les Journaux du Front*, a 1917 study that presents excerpts from nearly two dozen such publications of the trenches, the editor, Pierre Albin, noted,

Fig. 34. Icart and a compatriot pose before their World War I airplane.

Fig. 35. Icart in military uniform, probably taken before his assignment to flight duty, since the cap indicates assignment in the infantry.

"We were not discouraged at the Front. With confidence, we conserved our old French gaiety. We could not believe all had been lost. Courageously, we accepted the lengthy days and the harshness of the battle. We made ourselves at home. We published the magazines with their articles and verse. Without a doubt, they were not comparable to the pages of the immense *Temps* or the luxurious *Figaro*, but the verve and the spirit made us forget all the imperfections of the realization. For nothing was lost when we could see our gaiety reborn right in front of the enemy." [17]

Icart frequently drew incidental cartoons to accompany the text in the small magazine, works which continued to delight the men who read *L'Echo*.

Icart was soon bored with drawing maps from photographs taken by fliers over enemy territory. He asked permission to train for flight duty and his request was granted. He continued, however, to submit drawings and artwork for *L'Echo*. Icart became a member of the Tenth Army of the Air, and by the summer of 1916, he had his wings. An early photo shows Icart and a companion standing near the two-man plane he regularly flew over enemy territory (Fig. 34). Figure 35 shows Louis Icart in his military uniform.

A humorous look at his early flight training and his experiences as a flyer appears in the September 15, 1916, issue of *Fantasio*, the humor magazine that so intrigued him in his early years as an artist. The article, titled "How to Become an Ace," was Icart's tongue-in-cheek view of flight training. "It is not everything to get into the air," he wrote, "and to stay aloft despite the blows of the wind, the sudden eddies, the lift, etc. . . . everything is to descend again. For, according to Palisse, 'the higher the sky, the lower the earth.' " [18]

While this article was the only written material Icart supplied to *Fantasio*, he sent them abundant numbers of cartoons dealing with the war. His cartoons were a regular feature of *Fantasio*, *La Baïonnette*, and *Le Rire Rouge*, the wartime edition of *Le Rire*. These three magazines were strong morale boosters. The positive, always the positive, was the key thought behind French World War I periodicals. Designed to bring smiles in terrible times, these publications used satire as a salve for the damaged emotions and lives of the French people. The works of Louis Icart, Gerda Wegener, André Marty, and other humorists were vibrant with patriotic humor.

Many of the cartoons that Icart drew for these magazines would later be repeated as etchings. The December 16, 1915, issue of *La Baïonnette* features a full-color, full-page cartoon by Icart, *L'Amour des Ailes* (Love of the Wings; Fig. 36). A flyer, about to take off in his plane, kisses his ladylove farewell, calling her his "dove." This image was later used by the artist as a painting in 1922 and as an etching, *Avant le Raid,* 1925 (Fig. 37).

Men at war, however, were not the only subjects considered by Icart. *La Baïonnette,* which was published in an edition of 100,000 copies, published clever cartoons that were often insolently suggestive. In one Icart cartoon, two young women converse after the departure of a soldier on leave: "And what did he tell you about the war during his six days?" asks the one lady. "Oh," says the other in surprise, "I forgot to talk to him."

In all his cartoons Icart still stressed feminine beauty. Another cartoon from World War II, from *Fantasio,* displays a young woman who has taken the job of a subway conductor while he is away at war (Fig. 38). Her feminine charms, over and above her duty to her country, are inescapable.

The French humor magazines also participated actively in raising funds for the war effort and for charitable causes. *Le Rire Rouge* organized a large exhibit, le Salon des Humoristes, at the Palais de Glace in the winter of 1916. Another important exhibit, *La Guerre et les Humoristes,* was organized by the Société des Dessinateurs-Humoristes and the Société des Artistes-Humoristes to profit the cause of disabled artists and the families of artists killed in action. The exhibit at the Galerie la Boëtie, in March 1917, featured four etchings by Louis Icart among the 1,139 pieces on display.

The war was not always a time for humor, and Icart also produced passionate patriotic images that are today considered his most moving artistic expressions. The artist did not have access to etching materials at the front, but on his visits to Paris, he devoted as much time as possible to serious etchings on the war theme. Several galleries in Paris favored such patriotic creations since they sold well to a buying public that was brimming over with the anger and fever of the struggle.

One important artistic expression by Icart in this vein is *La Voix du Canon,* 1917 (Fig. 39). Without a doubt, it is the most unnerving work Icart ever created, and it ranks with his best creations. The fiery screaming figure of death in female form shoots from the French cannons with malevolence. The work so impressed a fellow soldier and poet, Pierre Lasseau, that he wrote the following poem "for Louis Icart in respectful homage from a poilu:"

THE VOICE OF THE CANNON

Criminals, stop your fiery battle.
Listen, o demons, to the voices of our cannons,
How they rush through the metal,
Listen and tremble, they have no names,
They have let go a cry of their burning rage.
It is a frightening cry that freezes you with horror.
Yes, it is a cry of death, coming for your feeble souls.
Yet it is a joyous cry which was locked in our hearts,
It is a cry of hosanna, it is a cry of victory,
It is a coarse word, even Glory shudders,
It is a triumphant cry which will never die,
For you are damned by the echoes of our fierce French cannons.[19]

Fig. 36. *L'Amour des Ailes* (Love of the Wings),
cartoon from *La Baïonnette,* December 16, 1915.

Fig. 38. *La Remplaçante,* cartoon from *Fantasio,* June 1916.

Fig. 37. *Avant le Raid* (Before the Attack), drypoint and etching, 1925, 21 x 17½.

Fig. 39. *La Voix du Canon* (Voice of the Cannon), drypoint and etching, 1917, 23 x 16, edition of 100.

The searing French patriotism in that poem equals the feeling in the etching, an extremely rare work which was limited to 100 copies by Icart. Such works helped to encourage soldiers at the battle lines and to strengthen the faith back home. As etchings of this type gained popularity in the French art galleries, artists from all over the country submitted works for the better galleries on the rue de Rivoli and rue Royale in Paris.

Such pieces, which had a great appeal in a country in the throes of war, became easily salable. In 1918, Icart created another World War I work, *Marianne, ou La Marseillaise* (Fig. 40), an etching that personified France with a large tricolor flag. This particular pose and figure was actually taken directly from a photograph of Mlle Delysia, a popular singer who sang the French national anthem in a revue in London. The photograph appeared in the March 1, 1915, issue of *Fantasio*, but the subject had greater impact as an etching. Icart created other works featuring patriotic women draped in the flags of their homeland, such as Miss Britannia and an American Miss Liberty. While Icart was at the front, Fanny submitted *Marianne* and other works to the various Paris galleries that had successfully sold his earlier creations. The war pieces particularly intrigued Mme Henaut, owner of Galerie Henaut at Place des Pyramides. For years, Mme Henaut had been exporting works by various artists to a gallery in Milwaukee, the F. H. Bresler Company, Inc. This firm, which had developed an exclusive clientele for French artwork in the Milwaukee area, welcomed any additions that Mme Henaut could provide. She told Fanny Volmers about the American gallery, and Fanny agreed to let her ship a number of early Icart etchings, among them *Marianne*, to the United States.

Another gallery that handled Icart's work was H. Wagram, a firm with extensive connections in the United States. Wagram had exported a few Icart etchings to

Fig. 40. *Marianne, ou La Marseillaise,* drypoint and etching, 1918, 12 x 19½.

associates in the United States and in England in 1913. At the time, the works, created while Icart was still oriented toward fashion design, had been purchased from him for export purposes, and they were not sold in the French galleries of Wagram or its affiliates. The pieces were copyrighted in the United States by the French firm. They were not especially popular, but even at that time there was enough of a market in this country for French graphics to stimulate continued exports.

H. Wagram was also the publisher of Icart's *Gestes de Femmes,* an unusual portfolio of twelve etchings that showed Frenchwomen at work during the war. Limited to 250 copies, the portfolio of etchings is among his strongest tributes to French glory. Such works, like most of the World War I etchings, were generally distributed only in France, but by the end of the war in November 1918, even the patriotic French had wearied of war-oriented themes, and the artist had to consider other subjects.

Icart returned from army life with the rank of major. Upon reentering civilian life, he found an eager market, primed for his etchings by Fanny's industrious representation. Galeries Wagram and Henaut both asked him to supply more etchings for the export trade. Their American distributors, generally galleries that sold popular, not fine, arts, had asked for more works of French "chic."

Fanny had changed little during Icart's absence. If anything, she became more youthful. Her golden curls, baby-doll lips, and wide expressive eyes were to appear in every new Icart etching. *Les Roses* (Fig. 41), a very romantic work, etched shortly after Icart's return from the war, pays homage to his lover. Fanny's look of childlike coquetry was well suited to works such as this one, and the figure at her feet, who probably represents Icart, is a man who cannot quite believe that this vision is actually his. As if she might vanish, he desperately grasps to hold on to her. This work, limited to 25 impressions, was Icart's first work in a new cycle. He had shifted from portraying

Fig. 41. *Les Roses,* drypoint and etching, circa 1920, 18 x 14½.

the grim images of the First World War to expressing a new appreciation of the Frenchwoman. But now his beauties were no longer fashion models. Their character and personality began to dominate. He idolized the Frenchwoman—her beauty, her coquetry, and even her innocent cruelty.

Other good news greeted Icart when he returned from the war. His first wife, having found a lover of her own, agreed to Icart's request for a divorce, and immediately thereafter he married Fanny.

In a few months Icart was so busy supplying etchings for the popular trade in the United States, that he had to hire the *atelier* of Pierre Gaudin to print them. Sales were healthy, and in 1920 Icart was financially stable enough to rent a larger studio and apartment on rue Emile Menier and to purchase a ten-acre estate at Itteville, forty kilometers south of Paris. The house was basically a three-room affair, and well suited for studio and living quarters. Fanny was delighted with the house because of the property surrounding it. She had always loved roses, and this house would give her the opportunity to cultivate them. Icart now had a much larger studio and he found room for a huge, hand-operated etching press (Fig. 42). They named the estate Maison de la Reine in honor of their daughter. Icart capped the prize with a shiny red Bugatti convertible, which he drove regularly to Paris on business.

The new country home encouraged Icart to continue painting when he was not working on copperplate. He was anxious to begin a new series of canvases, reminiscent of the golden Italian landscapes he had seen during the war. While his

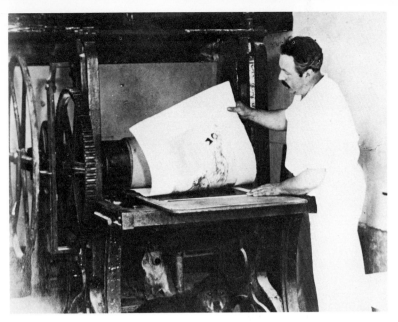

Fig. 42. Icart pulls a proof of *Joie de Vivre* from the etching press at Itteville. Companions watch from beneath the press.

subject matter had not changed—the eighteenth-century pastorale, landscapes, tales
from mythology, and the *commedia dell'arte*—these paintings began to take on a new
look. Infused with shades of gold, purple, and brilliant red, they were strongly
Impressionist in feeling. He would call this period *manière rouge* and the critics would
refer to him as "the painter of the golden palette." [20]

Shortly after settling in Maison de la Reine, Louis took Fanny to Italy for their
honeymoon. They fell in love all over again in the haunting cities of Venice and
Florence. The inspiration that Icart found here during the war came into brilliant focus
when he shared those cities with his beautiful wife.

The Icarts returned to Itteville and learned that Galèrie Simonson on rue
Caumartin was interested in sponsoring a one-man exhibition of Icart's oil paintings.
Icart selected twenty canvases from those he had painted in that last year, and on
March 11, 1920, Icart at last had his first one-man show in Paris. The critical response
was mixed. *Le Matin* raved about the exhibit, calling the luminous new works an
"outstanding revelation" [21] of new talent. *L'Oeuvre,* on the other hand, advised
Parisians to look in the window of the gallery, "shrug your shoulders and pass it
by." [22]

While the critics may not all have liked the new red tones found in Icart's
paintings, the customers of Galerie Simonson did; all the paintings were sold before
the exhibit ended.

Later that same year another Icart creation caused a small sensation at a special
exhibition called Le Salon de la Mode on rue Lapérouse. The Salon was instituted as
an annual exhibit of fashion designs by painters, etchers, sculptors, and other artists
who did not ordinarily earn their living in this field. Icart presented a bold wedding
ensemble made of white peacock feathers. The following year Icart contributed an
even more bizarre original to the same annual exhibit—a pair of arm-length gloves
made of real snakeskin. Two rubies adorned the top of each hand, giving a lady's arms
the illusory appearance of black-and-green serpents. Icart's two spectacular creations
were the most publicized features of the two exhibitions.

The artist enjoyed such occasional departures from the etching plate and the
canvas, but during the early Itteville years, Icart was generally too busy to produce
anything but etchings and paintings. Other Paris galleries had asked him to supply
them with etchings, and in 1921, L'Estampe Moderne, a publisher of the graphic arts,
and a major distributor of such works to America, asked Icart to supply them with a

sufficient quantity of etchings to meet the needs of their American gallery affiliates. L'Estampe Moderne supplied original works of art to the American decorator trade, those galleries that employed artwork as a decorative accent to a room, rather than as an individual artistic creation. In many ways, the etchings of Louis Icart—frivolous, saucy, and pretty—were well suited for this kind of market. Icart's etchings were an immediate success with American buyers. The works sold for ten to forty dollars each, and they were endlessly appealing, both in their variety and in their ability to meet any of the buyer's decorating needs.

L'Estampe Moderne, working with another Paris gallery that had been selling Icart's oil paintings, Galerie Manuel Frères, asked Icart if he would be interested in taking a publicity trip to the United States. A major exhibition of his work would be arranged in that country if he accepted. Icart's adventurous spirit would not allow him to turn down the offer, although he had to work hard to convince Fanny to go. Having found happiness in Itteville, she did not want to leave Reine for such a long period of time, but her duty to Icart and her dedication to his burgeoning career obliged her to go. Icart accepted the offer, and L'Estampe Moderne made arrangements for an American debut of Icart's paintings at the galleries of the Wanamaker department stores in New York and Philadelphia.

In the winter of 1922, Louis and Fanny Icart boarded the S.S. *La Savoie,* the huge French Line passenger steamer, for their first visit to the United States. Despite her initial reluctance to go, Fanny played her role well once the journey began. She and Louis were the gracious and delightful stars of the voyage, and they made many friends among the passengers, many of whom Icart later presented with original sketches that he had made while on board the ship. In exchange, some of their new friends offered thanks in the form of poems which Fanny carefully placed in a scrapbook of memories of the trip. Among the poems was one called *La Parisienne* by a M. Hinyant, a work which praised the wondrous charm and beauty of Icart's creations. A second glance at the three-stanza, rhymed poem reveals that the first letters of each line spell "Louis Icart, Merci." [23]

When *La Savoie* docked in New York, Rodman Wanamaker, president of the department stores, was there to greet the Icarts. With him was a press corps of admirable proportions, a credit to his effectiveness as a publicist, since many of the reporters had never heard of Louis Icart before. In fact, reporting the arrival, one of the news services referred continually to the couple as Mr. and Mrs. Ysart, an error that was repeated in newspapers all over the country.

Fanny created the greatest interest with her "sea veil," a new fashion design by her husband. An unusual, latticed shawl, the odd accessory was worn over the bottom portion of the face, much in the manner of the facial coverings worn by some Arabian women. Fanny's glorious eyes were thus accented, and the press showed more interest in her than in the artist or his works.

Icart's first American exhibition opened on November 27, 1922, at Belmaison, the fifth-floor art gallery of John Wanamaker's New York department store at Broadway and Ninth Street. The exhibit of fifty oils and fifty original sketches and etchings met with mixed degrees of favor from the critics.

On January 2 the exhibit moved to Wanamaker's Philadelphia store. "The paintings," read the catalog for the showing, "are done in a warm glow of golden red and orange lights reminiscent of the golden cities of Italy and Spain where Mr. Icart completed the development of his methods.... They suggest the spirited touch, sparkling color, and picturesque sketching of the Italian Guardi, and the delicate grace of the French Watteau, but a Watteau and Guardi modernized to the 20th century." [24]

Two of the paintings in the exhibit were portraits of French actresses, including Cecile Sorel, who had recently appeared in Broadway theatrical productions. The portrait of Mlle Sorel helped Icart obtain other commissions for completion in the United States. Interestingly enough, his fee was quite high for an artist whose works were just being featured in America for the first time. Said the New York *Herald*, "Louis Icart is the only painter known to have painted the life-size portrait in less time than it takes a photographer to develop and print a photograph. Shortly before coming to this country, Mr. Icart painted a portrait of Mlle Favart, the noted French actress. The portrait was executed in five hours for the sum of $3,000. The artist has been known to receive as much as $10 a minute for portrait commissions." [25]

One of Icart's first American portraits was that of the actress Lilyan Tashman. The artist later made plans to visit Hollywood, where he hoped to paint portraits of Pola Negri and Charles Chaplin, the latter being a performer Icart admired greatly. But the artist's time was spent exclusively on the East Coast and he never had the opportunity to visit Hollywood. As a subject for painting, however, New York City was sufficient for Icart. He described New York as a "fairyland of color and light," [26] and he painted several *manière rouge* studies of New York harbor, Times Square, and other famous Manhattan landmarks. A great lover of opera and classical music, Icart attended performances at the Metropolitan Opera House and at Carnegie Hall. He had nice things to say about *les femmes Americaines* as well. "In New York," he announced, "there are no old women.' " [27]

Fanny Icart found her own treasure on the journey, one she regarded with equal fondness—a rusty bundle of fur in the form of a Chow Chow, which she named, appropriately, "Dollar." Dollar, like many of the other Icart pets at Itteville, would become subject matter for the artist's etching plate (Fig. 43).

During the New York visit, Icart, through representatives of L'Estampe Moderne, made contact with galleries that had been selling his etchings. He inquired about their further needs, and everywhere he went, he received the same request: more of the same. Icart's naughty Parisiennes had captured the hearts and tastes of the public more effectively than any other artist whose works were being exported from Europe. Suggestions were made for subject matter: the famous operas, storybook characters, heroines from literature. Influenced by the American market, Icart planned to do his future work in copperplate.

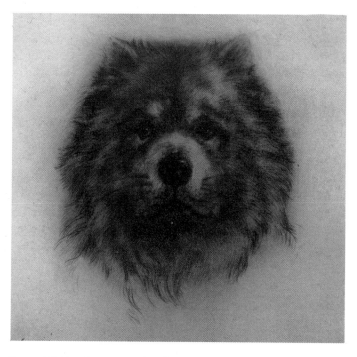

Fig. 43. *Dollar*, drypoint and etching, circa 1923, 8 x 8.

In June 1923, Louis and Fanny joined over three thousand other passengers on the Compagnie Générale Transatlantique French Line luxury liner *Paris* for the trip back home.

The weary travelers arrived at Maison de la Reine where they anticipated a life of quiet luxury. Icart began work on his new etchings, painting when he could find the time, but the demands of the eager American market, which he was anxious to cultivate, left him little time for painting. The artist found many of his ideas for etchings while sketching Fanny in her garden, which by now surrounded the Mediterranean-style home with a halo of color and fragrance. She cultivated roses, her favorite flowers, by the thousands, and the home was constantly alive with their perfume.

Icart's output was so great that another printer had to be hired to handle the overflow from the studio of Pierre Gaudin. Manuel Robbe *fils*, the son of the artist whose works had influenced Icart, had opened an *atelier* in Paris, where he printed etchings, lithographs, and other works for artists. Icart commissioned him to print etchings and he was so pleased with Robbe's work that he began to use him exclusively.

However, the increased business had certain disadvantages. Icart had to make frequent motor trips into Paris, each trip taking more than an hour's time, and this time spent traveling between Itteville and Paris began to distress him. Even on weekends, Icart and Fanny found themselves accepting dinner invitations from friends in Paris, and again they had to make the drive to the city. Fanny finally suggested moving back to Paris, but Louis wished to keep the country home. It would, he insisted, be perfect for weekends and occasional escapes from the frenzied Paris lifestyle. The Icarts agreed to maintain the Itteville home while living in a larger flat in Paris. By early 1925 they had found a spacious apartment at 112 Boulevard Malesherbes and the family of three returned to the "City of Lights."

The advantages of being in Paris again were immediately clear. Icart had access to the *atelier* of Manuel Robbe *fils* and he could now better supervise the preparation of his etchings. The several galleries that were now handling his works, including Les Gravures Modernes as well as Galerie Henaut and L'Estampe Moderne, were close at hand. Being in Paris also permitted the Icarts to strengthen their friendships with people they previously saw only infrequently, many of whom were prominent in the art world.

The French poet Audiberti was among Icart's closest associates and whenever they were separated, the two men engaged in thoughtful correspondence. Audiberti often defended his friend before the *Beaux-Arts*-oriented critics who did not favor Icart's work. His paintings, the poet once wrote, "belong so perfectly to the personality of our native land." [28] Audiberti was regarded as one of France's finest contemporary poets, and he respected Icart's poetic works. During their frequent correspondences, he encouraged the disciple of Victor Hugo to write as well as paint. Several years later, supported by such encouragement, Icart would do just that.

Another close friend was the novelist and historian Paul Yaki. Author of *Madame de Pompadour, La Belle Ferronière,* and other historical books, Yaki was best known for his books about Montmartre, Paris's colorful artists' quarter.

Gabrielle Claudine Colette, famous authoress of several novels, best known for *Chéri* and *Gigi,* was another noteworthy friend of the Icarts. She probably became acquainted with Icart when she was designing fashions. Icart's activities for various fashion houses no doubt put him in touch with the colorful Colette. Supposedly, Icart at one time painted a portrait of Colette, although no evidence of the work exists today; if it was indeed painted, it now remains well-hidden from public view, in a private collection. Colette was a great influence on Icart in that she encouraged him to illustrate his first *livre d'artiste*, a book whose illustrations were printed by some artistic medium, rather than by a photomechanical process, in a limited edition. The book was *L'Ingénue Libertine*, bearing the name Colette Willy as authoress. Originally, the work was two novels, *Minne* and *Les Egarements de Minne*, both written by Colette and her husband, Willy. It was mutually agreed that Colette combine the two works and the two names for a new edition. Icart provided illustrations for a limited edition printing of the "new" work, the first of more than two dozen books that would bear his illustrations after this successful experience.

Two years later, Icart illustrated another book for a friend, Abel Hermant, whose *Bigarrure* is an engaging collection of miscellaneous writings. Icart's illustrations were classic in feeling and etched in both color and black and white.

In 1930, Nouvelles Editions Excelsiors, a bibliophile society which specialized in the limited edition *livre d'artiste*, commissioned Icart to illustrate *La Fête Chez Thérèse* by Victor Hugo, in memory of the fiftieth anniversary of the writer's death. In 1934, Icart donated his artistic talents to *Jean Niquet*, a Christmas gift book that benefited the Children of Unemployed Artists and Writers, a Paris philanthropy.

Perhaps the most intriguing of Icart's friendships was with the young film actress, Mme Claudia Victrix. Besides Fanny, she is the only woman who appears recognizably in his etchings and paintings. In *Quatuor* (Melody Hour), 1934 (Fig. 44), Mme Victrix is clearly seen as the violinist on the far left.

Another of Icart's close friendships began in 1925 with Anton Schutz, the German engraver who came to the United States to study with Joseph Pennell. A brilliant businessman as well as a fine artist, Schutz was founder of the New York Graphic Society, a business enterprise that brought reproductions of art masterpieces into American homes. Shortly after Schutz founded the Society in the early 1920s, he contacted Icart and encouraged him to supply the firm with exclusive distribution

Fig. 44. *Quatuor* (Melody Hour), drypoint and etching, 1934, 23 x 18½.

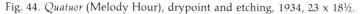

rights to his etchings in the United States. In exchange, Anton Schutz offered Icart the benefits of a sales operation that extended into all areas of the country. In a brilliant promotion idea, Schutz offered to establish a Louis Icart Society, and Icart would serve as president *in absentia*, while the business thrived with the guidance, and under the control of, the New York Graphic Society. Icart agreed, and the result was "Jazz Age" history. The etchings of Louis Icart had made a comfortable home for themselves in the United States, and buyers and collectors in all areas of the country cried out for more and more delightful French ladies.

Icart soon became recipient of another important honor when, in 1927, he was named a Chevalier of the French Légion d'honneur. The history of the Légion goes back to 1802 when it was instituted by Napoleon Bonaparte to honor those French citizens who, through their work, virtues, or talents, had contributed to the prosperity of the country. The President of the Republic serves as the *grand maître* of the Légion with various classes of membership beneath him. The corps of légionnaires comprises five classes: Chevalier, Officier, Commandeur, Grand Officier, and Grande Croix. Along with the honor, Icart was presented with the customary red ribbon that indicated his status as a Chevalier. The award had been given for Icart's various activities as etcher, painter, and designer, rather than for a particular creation or body of works.

The late 1920s were busy years for the Icarts. The artist devoted most of his time to producing etchings, which the United States markets would quickly devour. The artist preferred working at Itteville where atmosphere was peaceful and the water pure. Icart felt city water affected the quality of his etchings. Free hours were spent in painting subjects that were quite different from the playful pictures he provided for the popular markets. These unusual creations were deeply satisfying to him. While some critics had reproved him for his etchings, which they felt pandered to the requirements of the American decorative trade, Icart at times expressed the belief that professional jealousy at his financial success had encouraged negative reviews.

At Itteville, Dollar was joined by Vola, a sleek new greyhound, and later by a vast selection of other animals—borzois, dachshunds, a monkey, pigeons, and assorted poultry. Icart even kept two active beehives on the property since beeswax was an essential ingredient in the grounds he used for making etchings. The fresh honey supplied by the hives was equally valued when the artist or his wife tried their hands at cooking sweets and desserts.

With its peaceful rose gardens and a manmade lake which Icart had ordered for the property as a gift to Fanny, Maison de la Reine was well equipped to encourage his creative energies. Two metal sculptures of graceful swans, designed by Icart, floated in the lake, quiet and undisturbed by man or nature, forever beautiful.

Fanny, who now dressed in a wardrobe designed almost exclusively by her husband, spent much of her time posing for her husband, but she also found time to paint and sculpt, repeating, in many cases, works originally done as etchings by Icart. Sadly, Fanny's artwork lacked the vitality and technique inherent in her husband's work, but she painted only for her own satisfaction and had no intention of competing with him.

In this period of their lives, the Icarts one day received an unexpected visitor, Icart's old friend, Jules Esquirol. Esquirol, who was now editor of a French-language newspaper in Alexandria, Egypt, visited the Icarts at Itteville. It was his first meeting with Fanny, and he found her a "blond Greuze, blond with her large surprising eyes." [29] In Icart's studio, Esquirol found an even greater surprise:

A tormented Beethoven, striking the chords of his sonatas. Next a Christ, flagellating the merchants at the temple. On an easel, Lucrecia Borgia, beaten to death by her son, lifting eyes of terror onto her killer. And on all sides, the compelling canvases, everywhere . . . and what canvases, what colors, what violence. The red everywhere, it was an inferno.

"Have you abandoned your etchings? Your first grace? The caress of the Zephyr, the West Wind, to make place for a squall and a storm?"

Icart laughed heartily. His wife also, and they invited me into the second studio to see his press. He took out a carton. "Here, take this . . ." and I opened it to reveal his etchings. Years of creation, all carrying the inimitable signature of the artist who told me these works had been done several years before.

"And then?"

"Then, old man, this. This is it, and next, another thing. It is very simple. I have wanted to show those who distort me that I am not a slave, neither to a process nor to a method. That I etch that which *you* want—well called 'the grace'—but that I can also paint the suffering, the drama, and the thought-provoking, as well as the joy. Take that picture there, what do you think of that?"

I had before me a work representing a young woman in a light dress—oh so transparent—her arms about the mane of a black horse on a windy hillock [Fig. 45].

"Admittedly," said Icart, "when I create that, I satisfy the merchants. But there, in the other studio, I satisfy myself." [30]

In 1931 Fanny and Louis Icart made a major acquisition, a Romanticist's dream. At the auction gallery, Maison des Vents, Icart bid successfully for the complete letters of Juliette Drouet, many of which had been received at one time by Victor Hugo. "Juju's" faithful correspondence with the writer was conserved in an unsorted, haphazard manner. To Fanny, whose organizational abilities had already proved helpful to Icart, went the difficult task of classifying the letters—15,000 of them—a project that would take several years to complete. She would see her labors rewarded in 1943, with the publication of *La Servitude Amoureuse de Juliette Drouet à Victor Hugo* by Paul Souchon. Icart supplied the illustrations for this study of the letters, written by their friend Souchon.

Icart rarely exhibited at the Paris Salon, but in 1930, he unveiled a work that caused a sensation if not a scandal. *Méditation de Thaïs* (Fig. 46) was a huge nude portrait of Claudia Victrix as the exotic *femme fatale* of the Middle East. The painting was complete with Nubian slaves and the fiery red tones that had once been defined as "lurid" by an English critic.[31] While nudes were an acceptable entry in the Paris exposition, this was the first time that a prominent actress was recognizably painted in such a pose. The painting, however, rather than harming Mme Victrix's career, gave it an unexpected boost. In November 1933, she opened at the Théâtre Sarah Bernhardt in the coveted role of Marguerite Gautier in Alexander Dumas *fils*'s tragedy, *La Dame aux Camélias.* The role was highly prized by French actresses ever since it had been originated by *"la grande Sarah."* In a review of Mme Victrix's performance, *L'Illustration* said, "Mme Victrix, until now a professional singer and screen star, brings to the role of the immortal courtesan a warm conviction and her natural gifts of sensitivity and emotion." [32]

The play had a successful run, and Icart contributed a lithographic poster, measuring four by five feet, for the production. It is indeed surprising that Icart did not attempt more posters, for he had great respect for the art of poster design, a topic he discussed often with his friend Maurice Neumont, distinguished poster artist of early twentieth-century France.

Fig. 45. *Jeunesse,* drypoint and etching, 1930, 15½ x 24.

Fig. 46. *Méditation de Thaïs,* oil, 1930.

Fig. 47. The Neumont home on the Butte of Montmartre which Icart was determined to have for his own.

In addition to his love of poster art, Icart shared another fondness with his friend. Neumont lived in a magnificent house on the Butte of Montmartre (Fig. 47). The building intrigued and fascinated Icart. Seeing it for the first time from below on the rue Gabrielle, he is said to have remarked, "What a house for an artist. What a house for me! Someday I will own that house!" [33]

Indeed, in the late 1920s, Icart attempted to coax Neumont to give up the house, but as it was well suited to an artist, Neumont was not about to give it up. Sitting high above Paris on the same hilltop as Sacré Coeur, Place du Tertre, and other Montmartre landmarks, the five-story building seemed to perch dangerously on the edge of the Butte. The two-story edifice's windows facing the Paris skyline offered a spectacular view of the city, while allowing generous amounts of light to enter the third-floor artist's studio.

Reluctantly, Icart contented himself with his Boulevard Malesherbes flat, receiving a promise from Neumont that if and when the house was put up for sale, Icart would be the first to know. Maurice Neumont died in 1930, and a year later, Louis and Fanny again attempted to buy the house, although they had, in the interim, moved to larger quarters at 6 rue Jardin. The Montmartre house, however, was still unavailable.

Icart continued his etching work, but he engaged in other money-making activities. He drew advertisements for certain French winemakers such as Ayala and St. Raphaël Quinquina. He also increased his commissions for portraits, which were usually of actresses and politicians' wives, and he stepped up his export of etchings to the United States. During the mid- to late-1930s sufficient quantities of Icart etchings were available in the United States, but Icart was urged by the New York Graphic Society to continue production of fine pieces. Occasionally, the Society would exhibit Icart's oils and etchings in its New York showroom or in associated galleries and art shops in other parts of the country. Icart supplied the New York Graphic Society with the works they wanted and found he still had time for other activities, such as illustrating limited edition books.

The illustrated books that he did are unlike most found on public library shelves. It was in this medium that the artist could achieve his most imaginative erotic creations, and the result is a freedom of expression that is highly memorable. The artist worked closely with such bibliophile societies as Le Cercle Grolier, an organization with a membership of fifty, each of whom waited expectantly for the society's next erotic masterpiece.

Ever since the turn-of-the-century editor Ambroise Vollard had convinced the artist Pierre Bonnard to illustrate a deluxe edition of *Parallèlement* by Verlaine in 1900, the *livre d'artiste* had become an institution in France. Toulouse-Lautrec, Marc Chagall, Pablo Picasso, Raoul Dufy, and other prominent artists have all created such limited edition books containing original lithographs, etchings, or other works. While such fine book production was, of course, not unique to France, the *livre d'artiste* came into fullest blossom in that land. Today, the *livre d'artiste* is considered as valid a work of art as a painting or a series of etchings or lithographs.

Crebillon *fils*'s *Le Sopha* is one of Icart's most erotic works, a 1935 book with twenty-three original etchings. It was published in 1935 by le Vasseur et Cie., the firm that first proposed the idea to him and that limited the edition to 497 copies. Despite the fact that the book sold for 585 francs, a relatively large sum, the complete edition was sold out within a few months. This was partly due to the fact that it was peppered with amusing, highly erotic pictures. Icart and le Vasseur thereafter began work on the five-volume *Gargantua et Pantagruel* by François Rabelais, which featured seventy-six compositions by the artist. Lusty, bawdy, and definitely not for viewing by the general public, these volumes sold for the handsome sum of 1,875 francs. Interestingly enough, this was Icart's only work which employed photogravure and it was his most colorful creation to date. The edition was also large—976 copies—but its highly erotic contents soon found audiences all over France.

In book illustration, Icart had found a means of expression that did not restrict him. He was free to use any autographic process available to him, and he therefore experimented liberally in this medium. Until the Second World War, Icart devoted much time and energy to the production of his *livres d'artistes*, an output of nearly twenty works, including a one-of-a-kind volume, *La Femme de Marbre*, which he created exclusively as a gift for Fanny.

By the mid-1930s Icart had turned his artistic talents to another area. His poetic urges were brought to fruition in 1934 in the form of *Don Quichotte de la Manche*, a verse play in five acts. Written over a period of several years, the play emulated the work of both Victor Hugo and Edmond Rostand. Icart proved to be an agile poet, and the play contains many passages of beautiful verse. Though published in book form in 1934, *Don Quichotte* was not presented to an audience until April 23, 1938, when Cercle Molière, an amateur theatre group in Nice undertook the play at Le Casino Municipal de Nice. The production was so successful that it was repeated in December of that year. The play featured a cast of fifty with over one hundred costumes, five elaborate settings, and a live horse, all of which (excepting the horse) were designed by Icart.

Interestingly, in September 1938, the horse that had played the role of Don Quichotte's steed was taken ill. Icart, whose compassion for animals was inescapable, bought Rossinante from his owner for five francs, fifty centimes per kilo, and sent him to the Itteville estate for retirement. The presence of the horse at the Itteville home later inspired Icart to create the 1938 etching called *Pur-sang* (Purebloods, or Thoroughbreds) when it reached the United States (Fig. 48).

After the first performance of *Don Quichotte*, it was immediately evident that Icart's talents were myriad. "A sensational creation," said *Nice Eclaireur*.[34] The evening edition of the same newspaper, *Eclaireur du Soir*, declared, *"Don Quichotte* is its own proof. A veritable synthesis of all the gifts of its author, it contains a profusion of poetry, color, and humor. . . . this is well the most marvelous work that anyone has ever gleaned from the immortal Cervantes masterpiece." [35]

The critical response to this work so encouraged Icart that he began work on *Rabelais*, a longer verse play based on the life of the French satirist (1490–1553) widely known for his coarse, bawdy writings. *Rabelais* was eventually published in book form, but it never saw a stage production due to the interference of World War II.

Icart's artworks and creative writings put him in touch with many prominent artists, writers, and historians. Perhaps Icart's greatest weakness, after beautiful women, was food. Though he had been diagnosed as a diabetic in the early 1930s, he could not resist a platter of gourmet delights. His figure had already succumbed to the wages of overindulgence, but he ignored his doctor's advice and enjoyed fine foods and wines while he socialized with his contemporaries. While Fanny or the family cook gladly prepared meals for Louis and his guests, they would waive their rights to the kitchen on certain special occasions. Icart's culinary masterpieces were just cause for repeated visits to the Icart home by those who enjoyed evenings of fine food and philosophy.

Donning a white smock, different from the one he wore for painting, Icart could spend hours preparing special dishes for his gatherings of friends. His favorite creation was Coq d'Or, a capon in a golden jelly of orange and pineapple.

In 1937 Icart was elected a member of the *Club des Cent* (Club of the Hundred), an exclusive organization of gourmets—businessmen, artists, politicians, and famous chefs. Icart was a particular favorite with the membership for the clever menu covers he designed for the club's dinners. Women were not admitted to the gatherings, and this allowed the artist to produce etchings that were somewhat more erotic than those generally found on Parisian menus. When Icart's Coq d'Or was served at one *Club des Cent* dinner, he designed a menu of a nude servant girl with the golden dish in her arms as a nearby lecher looks on in admiration. The popular menu, which was limited to one hundred pieces, earned Icart the mock title, Chevalier de l'Ordre du Coq d'Or (Fig. 49).

The small paradise on earth that Louis and Fanny had created for themselves in Itteville and at rue Jardin began to crumble in May 1940, when German troops invaded France from the north. Horrible tales of German mass executions, rapes, and pillage spread quickly through the northern provinces of France. The panic was in part based on fact, but it was also generated purposely by the Germans, who knew that a frightened, panic-stricken civilian population would certainly hamper the fighting ability of the French Army. Literally millions of persons fled their homes in the North to enter Paris, the only place they imagined they would find safety. This series of events led to *L'Exode* (the Exodus), an event of great importance in French history. By the time the Germans moved into Paris on June 11, 1940, over one-quarter of the entire

Fig. 49. *Club des Cent* menu, drypoint and etching, circa 1937, 6 x 7½.

Fig. 48. *Pur-Sang* (Purebloods; Thoroughbreds), drypoint and etching, 1938, 35 x 18.

French population—8 million people—had been dispersed, and nearly half of the French military had been killed or taken prisoner by the Germans.

Icart was so moved by this series of events that he created *Croquis de l'Exode* (Impressions of the Exodus), an outstanding series of fifty monotypes that depicted the horrors of the route to Paris. In October of that same year, Icart submitted the works to *l'Illustration* magazine for possible publication. From the editor, R. Bascher, he received the only possible answer:

> I am returning your very interesting monotypes on the Exodus. As I had mentioned to you, it is perhaps not a question of reproduction so much that as long as the German occupation continues, their censorship forbids all references to the war. When we regain our liberty, however, we hope to publish several numbers concerning our disasters, and this will be the occasion for publishing several of your sketches, which are certainly gripping, moving, and of the highest artistic merit.[36]

Another serious effect of the Occupation was the interruption of the continued export of Icart's works to the United States. Once German troops moved into France, the United States immediately ceased all trade with France. As a result, the Louis Icart Society had to close its doors. While his financial position was strong, Icart had to face yet other disappointments. Copper for etching plates was impossible to obtain, and he had to melt down his canceled plates if he was to do any etching at all. Of course, the demand for Icart's works had decreased considerably, now that the American market was no longer available to him.

But the war hit the Icarts directly in July 1940, when an ominous letter arrived at their Paris apartment.

> MEMO: This is a copy of a letter from German soldiers who are occupying a villa at Itteville, in which there hangs a painting, which shows German soldiers brutally separating French civilians from their families during the First World War.
>
> To the absent proprietors:
> In Germany you will not find such hateful paintings. What do you think about the young German girls who violently lost their lovers during the occupation of the Rhine? Or about those thousands of Germans who died of starvation between the time of the Armistice and the signing of the Peace, 1918–19, whose tombstones could be inscribed "victims of the hatred of the conquerors"? You would prefer perhaps a more modern painting, where, under the protection of the French and English soldiers, you could admire the bestial assassination of uncountable Germans by the Polish military?
> Hang your painting then, if it gives you pleasure—Poor, Grand Nation.[37]

The note was signed "Your German occupiers." The thought of *les boches* at Maison de la Reine infuriated Icart and, despite protests from his wife and daughter, he raced to his country home. If the other Frenchmen would not stand up to those devils, he certainly would! But when he arrived he found the house empty and untouched. The caretaker then revealed that the Germans had changed their mind about using the house as lodgings, since there were too many of them and the three rooms, though large, were insufficient for their needs. Determined to prevent any further trespassing on his property, Icart moved his personal belongings to Itteville where he spent most of his time during the war. In a grim, symbolic gesture, he renamed the Itteville home Maison du Silence, vowing not to change the name again until the end of the German Occupation.

At Itteville, most of Icart's time was spent in painting. He had by now used up his reserve of copper for etching plates and so he turned to oil. The first project was a series of fifty canvases of *L'Exode*. He well knew that they would not be seen in an occupied Paris. Perhaps they would never be seen at all, but as an artist, and especially as a French artist, he had to put the works on canvas. In truth, these paintings were never displayed publicly; after the war, they were set aside by an Icart who was more eager to reestablish the American market for his etchings. However, among his paintings, they are his most sincere expressions. Historically, they represent possibly the only works of art that recorded the Exodus, an event in French history that was too easily forgotten in the shadow of the other horrors of World War II.

Icart's second project at Itteville was the continuation of a series of oils that had come to be known as *les visions blanches*. During the 1930s he had discovered a new technique that took his palette from the dominant red tones of the 1920s canvases to a pure, luminous interplay of delicate whites and grays, accented with pastel pinks and blues. The subject matter for *les visions blanches* was generally that of the etchings, but the technique, somewhat similar to that of the painter Eugène Carrière, was decidedly Impressionistic.

In 1943, 1 Place du Calvaire, his Montmartre dream, became available and Icart used the savings he had accumulated to buy the house. After they moved, to commemorate the new quarters, Icart designed a crystal chandelier in the form of a clipper ship, which was used to adorn the center of a third-floor studio (Fig. 50). Fanny turned the terraced garden into a rainbow of color. The Icarts had at last found their true home, a magical castle at the highest point in Paris.

At the conclusion of World War II, Icart was again able to purchase materials for etching, and he began immediately to create works for the American market. Always experimenting, Icart began to infuse his etchings with the same impressionistic quality as the oils he had recently completed. While he was pleased with the results, which were primarily created with an aquatint process, the markets responded negatively. Postwar etchings, like *Promenade aux Bois* (Springtime Promenade; Fig. 51), somehow did not have the same appeal. Anton Schutz and the New York Graphic Society, who began reimporting Icart etchings after the war, tried to revitalize American interest in the artist. In a daring public relations scheme, the Society encouraged the Icarts to visit New York once again to promote a touring exhibition of *les visions blanches*. Reluctantly, Icart made the journey to the United States. In December 1948, the series of paintings went on display at the New York Graphic Society showrooms in New York City.

America was at this time in no mood to accept pretty, elegant pictures from France. The country had just fought a long and costly war. Such flighty fantasies were inappropriate, and generally the critics chose to ignore the exhibits in New York and, later, in Philadelphia where they were seen at the Wanamaker department stores. Icart did not stay this time for a six-month visit to New York. Repeated indulgence in the wrong pleasures had made living with diabetes more difficult than ever for Louis Icart. Fanny had developed rheumatism, and at times she was in great pain. After four weeks, he returned to his home.

Icart, who could no longer find satisfaction in his work, perhaps because of his rejection in the United States, began to seek wonder cures for his ailments. He went to the spa at Vichy in hopes that the reviving waters there would give him the energy to continue his artistic endeavors. Instead, he returned to Paris in a worse state of mind, feeling helpless and burdensome to his wife.

On December 30, 1950, two days before the New Year celebration, Louis Icart

Fig. 50. The magnificent interior of 1 Place du Calvaire, Icart's Montmartre home. The paintings and the chandelier were all created by the artist.

Fig. 51. *Promenade aux Bois* (Springtime Promenade), drypoint and etching, 1950.

died quietly in his sleep at his Montmartre home. He was buried in a small cemetery not far from the Itteville home he loved so much. Fanny sold the Itteville estate not long after Louis's death, and lived at the Montmartre house until her death in 1971. Her remaining years were spent in concluding the private business affairs of her husband, in continued study of the letters of Juliette Drouet, and in quiet painting. She is buried in her family tomb in Bagneaux.

In her final creative works, Fanny attempted to emulate her husband's technique and imagination, but though she sold her works privately or gave them to friends, galleries did not exhibit them. In her last years, she would think often of her husband's vibrant, laughing face which had made their life together as nearly perfect as a storybook romance. She often spoke of his dedication to his work and expressed few regrets about their final separation. She realized that the years they spent together were magical, exciting years. The memory of their happiness together sustained her until her death.

Until recently, Icart's name was not widely known in modern France. Like many of his contemporaries, he was quickly forgotten. His effervescent carefree ladies had found their greatest market in the United States. But even in this country he has been only recently remembered. Ironically, it may have been the philosophy that directed his art that so effectively erased him from the public memory. He achieved his goals perhaps too well:

"I hold that a picture should be a source of dreams," he once said. "It should give diversion and repose to the troubled and life to the materialistic. It should be, as expressed by Camille Mauclaire, a book that one reads at a single glance." [38]

Fig. 52. *Werther*, drypoint and etching, 1928, 13 x 20.

CHAPTER 2

ELEGANCE IN COPPER

IN AMERICA, ICART ONCE SAID, "THE ARTIST IS WELCOMED AS AN EQUAL, AS WELL BY THE intellectual, the industrialist, or the financier. For in that land of producers, the artist is also seen as a producer, and it is by natural consequence that he may search for ways to sell his product without having to excuse himself." [39]

Icart's great appeal to popular American tastes was in defiance of many French art critics who viewed the United States as a fine arts wasteland, and while his exports helped to make him one of the wealthiest artists in France, they likewise placed him in a position of low regard among contemporaries. Creating art for profit was unthinkable to many French purists, and Icart was often criticized for this reason.

Yet Icart continued to defend his "commercial" art, at the same time continuing to produce paintings and book illustrations of a fine arts nature that were not meant for the popular buying market. This is not to say that his etchings were abbreviations of his full talents; the artist was as sincere about the workmanship in these "commercial" works as he was about other, more personal creations. Whether creating an etching for public distribution or an oil painting as a gift for Fanny, the artist put his full talents to work.

Surely in the United States between the two world wars, no "excuse" was necessary for the burgeoning business of "bedroom art" that Icart launched. The American market was ripe for decorative artworks from France and, in the years of their vogue, several hundred thousand impressions of his etchings were exported to America. Though possibly not as prevalent in American homes as the "art prints" of the great masters, whose works were reproduced by the millions via four-color reproduction processes, Icart's etchings had a similar popular appeal—only with a bonus: Icart's etchings were *original* works of art, printed under the artist's supervision and hand-signed by their creator.

Icart's etchings were also reasonably priced, placing them within the budgets of middle-class Americans. A 1932 Louis Icart Society catalog lists most available Icart etchings at twelve to fifteen dollars each, with a few pieces selling for up to twenty dollars. Add to this their French origin, a Continental touch so important to those Americans who wanted their tastes to be identified with Paris chic, and the artist's creations constituted a highly salable package.

Some may wonder how Icart's etchings managed to maintain their appeal to American buyers during the Depression. Although few people could afford the luxury of a fifteen-dollar picture, enough Americans still had the wherewithal to purchase Icart's lighthearted artworks. Admittedly, many buyers of fifteen-dollar etchings had previously been buyers of more expensive works of art, and Icart's charming ladies were an economical answer for households that struggled to maintain a sense of levity in such lean times. *Werther,* 1928 (Fig. 52), and *La Cigarette* (Memories), 1931 (Fig. 53), typify the humor and elegance found in many of his etchings.

Icart's etchings were of the same frivolous nature as many of the Hollywood films of the same era. Indeed, the identity was so strong that one critic estimated that "... seven out of ten domestic interiors in Hollywood productions are graced with Icarts...." [40] *Parfum de Fleurs* (Love's Blossom), 1937 (Fig. 54), and *Le Sofa,* 1937 (Fig. 55), are among several etchings that capitalized on American tastes for Hollywood glamour. At the same time there is a wry element of humor that pervades the works, and the viewer wonders whether he is meant to take all that extravagant luxury seriously. This underlying humor is characteristic of many Icart etchings produced for the American market. A common reaction on first seeing an Icart etching is a knowing smile; the viewer spots those familiar attributes of French jest: the partially exposed bosom; the look of innocence combined with worldliness; the wind-blown skirt that shows just a little too much thigh; a playful pet that causes an excess of his mistress's *déshabillé.* Obviously, the etchings that the artist exported to the United States were in no way meant to portray a serious picture of Frenchwomen. They were intended to be decorative, and Icart made no secret of it. Somber, serious works, etchings permeated with meaning or symbolism, would not have sold with the same rapidity. The artist gave his admiring public a skillfully executed, pretty picture for the right spot on the wall and at the right price. Hence his success in the competitive American market.

During the peak of his career, Icart found ideal working conditions at Itteville. There, in the studio facing east, he worked at a large table outfitted with a transluscent screen to soften the glare from the sunlight on his copper engraving plate. From the large window he observed Fanny in her gardens or playing with one of the pets that populated the estate. Frequently, her daily activities were the subject matter of his etchings.

Using pencil or crayon, the artist would make several quick sketches of Fanny in a particular pose or situation, eventually honing down the series to one final sketch that would indicate the shape and colors to be used in the completed etching. By the time the idea had been taken this far in the artist's mind, few variations in color or design appeared in the final product. *Paresse* (Laziness), 1925, is shown in the final artist's

Fig. 53. *La Cigarette* (Memories), drypoint and etching, 1931, 18 x 15.

Fig. 54. *Parfum de Fleurs* (Love's Blossom), drypoint and etching, 1937, 25 x 17.

Fig. 55. *Le Sofa,* drypoint and etching, 1937, 25 x 17.

sketch before engraving (Fig. 56) and in the completed etching form (Fig. 57). Few stylistic changes appear in the final product except, of course, the reversed image.

A diligent, determined worker, Icart could often complete an etching plate within a day's time. Most pieces, however, because they did require using various techniques, took about a week to complete. From the outset of his career, Icart knew that the results he wanted were best achieved by employing a variety of mediums. Rather than limiting his efforts to drypoint, aquatint, or soft-ground etchings exclusively, he generally employed all these techniques in each work.

Icart's intaglio work may be divided into two types: acid etchings and drypoints. In the former process, a zinc or copperplate is coated with an acid-resistant substance called a ground. The image is incised into the ground with a variety of tools, and after the drawing is completed, the entire plate is immersed in an acid bath which eats away those areas of the plate that are no longer protected by the ground. When the plate is later inked and wiped clean, ink remains in the incised lines cut by the acid. To make individual impressions, dampened paper is placed against the metal plate on a special etching press which runs both pieces between rollers under great pressure. The press forces the paper into the lines of the etching plate, thus picking up the inks in the form of the completed image.

Drypoint employs basically the same principle, but the process eliminates the need for acid because the artist incises the image directly onto the plate with sharp engraving needles and other tools. In either method, once the basic image has been obtained, a variety of textures, tones, or color formations may be incorporated into the work by employing aquatint, a method that uses an acid-resistant resin dust. Use of the resin dust in varying quantities on different areas of the plate allows the artist to

Fig. 56. Pastel sketch for the etching *Paresse* (Laziness), 1925.

Fig. 57. *Paresse* (Laziness), drypoint and etching, 1925, 19 x 15.

determine the amount of tonal gradations that will appear in the completed work. While Icart employed both methods in his etchings, he usually depended on drypoint for the basic image.

Icart used two distinct methods for coloring his etchings. The simplest, though most time-consuming method, required hand-coloring each etching after it was printed. During the early part of his career, Icart performed this task himself, but as the demand for additional works grew, taking up more and more of his time, the hand coloring was left to skilled art printers, who worked under his careful supervision. Coloring a work with so many small areas, such as the feathery costumes in *Folies*, 1935 (Fig. 58), is no small task. While the flesh tones were colored with the plate method, one of Icart's printers reported that coloring by hand the rest of the prints in the edition required several days' work. *Folies* is one of the later etchings partly colored by hand. *Can-Can*, 1935 (Fig. 59), a work on a similar theme, was colored with plates.

Color plates—anywhere from one to three—were the most commonly used method of coloring the etchings. Icart would acid etch the color plates, using aquatint, feathering, sugar lift, and stippled grounds to create the various textures and tonal effects he wanted to achieve through color. When, for example, only one color was to be used in an etching, as in *Werther* (Fig. 52), a 1928 work which depicts Lotte, the gracious beauty of Jules Massenet's opera, the colored ink was applied to a second plate which had been prepared for printing via the aquatint method. The finished drypoint was run through the press another time, this time carefully registered to align with the new copperplate which applied the color impression. Because the paper was dampened before each printing, speed was essential lest the size of the paper change too quickly for a successful registration.

In some instances, several colors could be applied to one color plate. This method, known as *à la poupée*, required working several colors into separate areas on the plate with small pieces of felt or with the fingers. Since each impression required a reinking of the color plate, variances in color intensity occurred from etching to etching. The use of several color plates with varying numbers of colors on each, along with added hand coloring, gave works like *Le Bouddha en Colère*(The Angry Buddha), 1926 (Fig. 60), and *A la Fête* (Mardi Gras), 1936 (Fig. 61), their distinctive vitality.

Icart mixed his own colored inks using various colored powders and special oils. Early impressions of some works gave Icart and his printers great opportunity to experiment with color. An early impression of *Dame aux Camélias*, 1927 (Fig. 62), a work inspired by the French actress Claudia Victrix and her role in the Dumas play, shows the heroine in a gown of deep lavender. Requests by some American galleries for pictures with more pink tones, however, encouraged Icart to prepare the work in the more conventional pink, a color which, unfortunately, detracts from the rich, deep beauty of the original. The galleries were right, however; *Dame aux Camélias* was one of the most popular Icart etchings produced during the 1920s, and over a thousand impressions were made of the work.

Some Icart etchings were available in a choice of colors. The nude seen in *Modèle I*, 1932 (Fig. 63), could be obtained either as a blonde or as a brunette.

Some of the techniques Icart employed in his graphic work, while not entirely new, were rarely used at the time. Generally, he would engrave the drypoint image first, then, after protecting the drypoint features of the plate with varnish, he would acid etch the backgrounds. *Conchita*, 1929 (Fig. 64), employs a stippled-ground technique Icart called "grain of resin." After mixing a solution of denatured alcohol and colophony powder, Icart created a syrupy substance that he painted onto the copperplate. He then heated the plate, which evaporated the alcohol, leaving only the hardened ground, which cracked into tiny wrinkles or "grains." Into these areas Icart drew details of the background with a soft pencil. After immersing the plate into acid, the irregular background patterns he favored would form. The veil that partially obscures the dancer's nude body was created by this stippled-ground effect. *Conchita*, one of the most provocative nudes Icart every produced for the export market, features the heroine of the Pierre Louÿs story, "Woman and Puppet," who shames her lover by appearing in a suggestive nude dance in a bistro. Icart's brilliant use of coloring and shading to give the effect of stage lighting, and the realistic figure with her stoic expression, makes this one of his most dramatic etchings. As would be expected, the blatant nudity—specifically unhidden pubic hair—offended many potential American buyers, and *Conchita* was a poor seller. The same scene is also the subject of a large oil painting by Icart featuring the same woman. In the painting, however, Icart added the audience—an ugly, raucous collection of clapping and whistling male admirers.

The more gracious *La Peigne Espagnol* (Spanish Shawl) circa 1922 (Fig. 65), shows how Icart applied ground to achieve an interesting background effect. Icart's deft use of technique to achieve the lace pattern in the fan and the delicacy of the shawl makes this one of his most sensitive portraits. A similar effect is seen in the raincoat in *L'Averse* (Rain), 1925 (Fig. 66).

Another technique, known as feathering, allowed Icart to acid etch only certain areas of a copperplate. Into drops of water on the plate, Icart would add etching acids, blending the two by moving the mixture across the area with a feather. Icart used this technique to create the unusual washlike backgrounds that characterize many of his works. Sometimes the artist would highlight the background areas by impressing leaves or branches of ferns into the grounds on an etching plate. These impressions are clearly seen in the screen pictured in *Les Orchidées* (Orchids), 1937 (Fig. 67), a work which suggests the image of a giant orchid when turned upside down. *Les Orchidées* and its companion piece, *Les Lis* (Lillies), 1934 (Fig. 68), were among several Icart etchings that were varnished after printing. Because of the subtleties in each work, the artist felt that a coat of gloss varnish would highlight the background areas.

Another process, sugar lift, was occasionally employed by the artist to achieve such features as the lacy dress pattern in *Le Poème* (Fig. 13). A sugar solution, or even saliva, acting as a neutralizer, is mixed with acids on the plate. Uneven biting results, and complex spatterlike patterns are formed.

A great proponent of using the best possible materials, as well as an active experimenter, Icart spared no expense in his selection of tools and supplies. From the beginning of his career, he preferred copperplates to those of iron, which were also in use at the time. The copper was much more receptive to fine line work, and, later in Icart's career, when electroplated with nickel, it was able to sustain greater numbers of impressions. The artist's engraving needles varied in thickness and shape, allowing him to create lines of varying thicknesses. Their points were made of diamond, the hardest substance known to man, a necessity for an artist who used so many fine lines to create his images.

In a lengthy article on his etching techniques, appearing in the short-lived trade journal *Pictures and Decoration,* Icart discussed the various uses for his many etching points:

> The point must sense its way through the waves of the hair, the molding of a leg, and as for the clothing, the general movement of the body. This first phase of the work gives a sort of monotonous gray outline, but the practiced hand is able to put "feeling" into the plate.
>
> Now for the accents or the high spots. For this purpose, I select those points used for specialized work. For example, this one, so very sharp, is able to scratch in the waves and curls. The deepness of the incision in the metal depends upon whether I wish to depict a blonde or brunette. The deeper the cut, the greater the accent. The deepness of the cut determines the shadings in an etching and therefore special emphasis must be made on this point.
>
> In picturing bare flesh, I must use a more rounded and shorter point so as to give the face, arms, and legs the desired shadings and velvety softness. When a face is well done in drypoint, it seems as though the subject had just finished powdering her nose.[41]

The number of impressions made of each Icart etching for eventual distribution may never be known since edition sizes were determined by current demand for a particular work. For example, a 1922 catalog of L'Estampe Moderne, a French

Fig. 58. *Folies,* drypoint and etching, 1935, 25 x 15½.

Fig. 59. *Can-Can Française* (French Quadrille), drypoint and etching, 1935, 25 x 15½.

Fig. 60. *Le Bouddha en Colère* (The Angry
Buddha), drypoint and etching, 1926.

Fig. 61. *À la Fête* (Mardi Gras), drypoint and etching, 1936, 18½ x 18½.

Fig. 62. *Dame aux Camélias* (Lady of the Camelias), drypoint and etching, 1927, 21 x 17.

distributor of Icart's etchings, lists forty-two etchings by the artist, including several early works originally published by Galerie Georges Petit in 1911 and 1914, as well as l'Estampe Moderne works published in 1919. These works were strictly limited to editions of three hundred each. Thereafter the copperplates were canceled by the artist who incised a large "X" across the front of the image, preventing the making of additional impressions. After 1922, however, when Icart made his first journey to the United States, he made numerous contacts with American galleries and art shops who were anxious to have as many etchings as he could supply. After the Louis Icart Society was formed several years later, it issued trade catalogs of Icart's works, which were distributed all over the nation, and galleries ordered large quantities of selected etchings. While attempts were made to assure buyers of the limited edition aspect of the works, the etchings were, in truth, produced as demand for them was received. Beginning in 1925, three hundred was still the basic number of impressions made of each Icart etching, but the plates were not destroyed as previously, and if the call for additional pieces was sounded loudly enough, the artist and his printers thought nothing of printing additional impressions. Many of Icart's copperplates were now electroplated with steel or nickel after completion, a process that allowed him to make sizable numbers of impressions. He was delighted that some works were so popular and that hundreds of people enjoyed them. Consequently, after 1925, Icart rarely numbered his etchings. Works which were truly limited editions were marked with the number of the impression and the size of the edition, but these were generally works that were not intended for United States distribution and not handled through regular channels. Usually made as gifts for friends or as limited editions for special groups of French collectors, these pieces were often kept to as few as fifty impressions. The penciled numbers or letters, which may appear in the lower left margin of some Icart etchings, generally refer to catalog designations or are geographical-distribution

Fig. 63. *Modèle I* (My Model), drypoint and etching, 1932, 16½ x 21.

codes. During this most popular period of his career, Icart felt that his work was not being overproduced or misrepresented as long as he did not indicate the size of the editions on the works.

Icart's remarkable success was not a spontaneous thing. Like most successful artists, Icart had to develop both a style and a technique during the early part of his career before finding the success in the competitive commercial art market.

In the early 1900s Icart's etchings clearly reflected the influence of his career as a fashion illustrator. His models wore the very latest in French *haute couture,* and the etchings were little more than studies of French fashion designs. Typical of these early works is *Coursing* (Fig. 69), a 1914 work that features a fashionably dressed lady with a large borzoi hound. The word "coursing" actually implies speed and movement, but it may also refer to a form of hunting where quick, sleek dogs seek out their prey.

Works like *Vision Printanière* (Vision of Springtime), 1914 (Fig. 70), and *Premiers Beaux Jours* (First Beautiful Days), 1914 (Fig. 71), are typically devoid of much character, yet show Icart's early emphasis on clothing, hats, and accessories such as parasols and feathers.

Icart's first major opportunity for professional development came with the First World War, when he used his talents as an etcher to produce powerful war-related statements. The artist's direct involvement put him in close touch with the French war effort and gave him firsthand insight into the kinds of imagery that would both please and inspire his countrymen. Each of the popular French artists of the period who

Fig. 64. *Conchita*, drypoint and etching, 1929, 14 x 21.

Fig. 65. *La Peigne Espagnol* (Spanish Shawl), drypoint and etching, circa 1922.

Fig. 66. *L'Averse* (Rain), drypoint and etching, 1925, 14 x 18½.

Fig. 67. *Les Orchidées* (Orchids), drypoint and etching, 1937, 19½ x 28.

Fig. 68. *Les Lis* (Lilies), drypoint and etching, 1934, 19½ x 28.

produced similar works had recognizable trademarks. The works of Francisque Poulbot generally featured wide-eyed waifs against a backdrop of war-torn villages. Adolphe Willette specialized in grotesque caricatures of the enemy. And Abel Faivre idealized the French fighter in glorious victories over the German challengers.

Icart, true to his innate instincts, made women the focal point of all his war pieces. In these remarkable etchings, his women are no longer mannequins, but symbols of a France fighting for her life. In *La Grenade* (The Human Grenade), 1918 (Fig. 72), the earth explodes around the feet of a beautiful nude. She lifts her arms to her fiery hair, from which the laurel leaves fly. Even in this early stage of his career, Icart made generous use of feathering and other special techniques to achieve a dramatic textured background in his work.

L'As Vainqueur (Winged Victory), 1918 (Fig. 73), even more symbolic than *La Grenade,* is one of the artist's most colorful World War I etchings. Created in honor of the French war ace, Captain Georges Guynemer (1895–1917), who singlehandedly downed fifty-four German planes before he was killed in action, *L'As Vainqueur* shows a German plane falling in flames beneath the victorious French biplane. The symbolic beauty who floats calmly above the violent scene wears a garment forming graceful wings bearing the blue, white, and red symbol of French aviation. In her hand, she carries the traditional laurel wreath of peace.

Le Coursier en Colère (The Angry Steed), 1918 (Fig. 74), shows an angry Miss France charging her war horse through a battlefield, holding a shredded German flag high over her head in arrogant victory. This exciting work shows an aspect of Icart's talent that was rarely revealed to his American buyers.

Another interesting war etching, *Défense de Foyer* (Defense of the Homeland), 1917 (Fig. 75), contrasts the image of a mother feeding her baby with the image of a French soldier at the front.

In 1917, while the war fires still raged, Icart readied *Gestes de Femmes* (Chronicles of Women), a portfolio of twelve small etchings, limited to 250 impressions each, depicting Frenchwomen from all walks of life in the roles they played during World War I. In this sensitive series, Icart focused on the realities of war, abandoning the symbolism seen in most of his other war etchings. Icart had no doubt seen a special issue of *La Baïonnette* called "Les Remplacantes," November 15, 1915, in which several artists recorded the activities of Frenchwomen who had replaced their fighting men in various civilian jobs. Icart did not submit works to this particular issue of *La Baïonette,* but he borrowed freely the ideas it presented.

Gestes shows the Frenchwoman as a munitions worker, as a nurse (Fig. 76), a farm worker, and as a conductress in the Paris Métro. His heroines give moral support to their men at war with a prayer in church, a package or letter from home, and dutiful study of a map of the front lines. Icart honors the mother who bids a final farewell to her son (Fig. 77), as well as the widows who lost their husbands in the fighting. He depicts the violence of the war in the villages (Fig. 78), and he also draws a symbolic Alsace-Lorraine (Fig. 79), the region of France that lost her freedom to Germany in 1871 (restored by the Treaty of Versailles in 1919).

These twelve pieces were etched with drypoint; aquatint was employed for gray tones and coloration. The artist also created an additional fifty portfolios in which he incorporated *remarques,* original pencil and watercolor sketches placed at the bottom of each plate, small pictures which expanded on the main scene. For example, in the scene of the women running from the German invaders (Fig. 78), the *remarque* shows the bloodied body of one of the women, who has just been shot by a German soldier.

Fig. 69. *Coursing,* drypoint and etching, 1914, 16 x 11½.

Inclusion of *remarques* was a common practice of many graphic artists of the time, and Icart used them most effectively in *Gestes.*

Because of the larger editions of later etchings, Icart, with a few exceptions, abandoned the practice of including *remarques.* When they are found on later etchings prepared for the popular market, they represent an afterthought, possibly added as a gift for a friend or as an additional personal "signature" for a particular buyer.

Another World War I etching is *Dans les Tranchées,* 1918 (Fig. 80), a work that sets a nubile Miss France against a backdrop of barbed wire in a bullet-cratered trench. The symbolic figure, who is again draped in a sash of blue, white, and red, offers a courageous French *poilu* a final kiss before he enters the battle.

After the First World War, the flavor of Icart's etchings changed once again. The artist relaxed his partriotic stance and began to create works that emphasized the beauty of Frenchwomen. Icart used Fanny as his model for most of the new creations, and rarely have an artist and model blended so well. At varying times, Icart interpreted her as a blonde or brunette, as a simple peasant girl, or as an elegant eighteenth-century lady. But whatever the costume, the color of the hair, or the situation, his etchings were clearly of Fanny, inimitably Fanny.

Fig. 70. *Vision Printanière* (Vision of Springtime), drypoint and etching, 1914, 11½ x 18½. (Collection of the Library of Congress)

Fig. 71. *Prèmiers Beaux Jours* (First Beautiful Days), drypoint and etching, 1914, 9½ x 15½. (Collection of the Library of Congress)

Fig. 72. *La Grenade* (The Human Grenade), drypoint and etching, 1917, 13 x 17½.

Fig. 74. *Le Coursier en Colère* (The Angry Steed),
drypoint and etching, 1918.

Fig. 73. *L'As Vainqueur* (Winged Victory), drypoint and
etching, 1918, 15 x 21½.

Fig. 75. *Défense de Foyer* (Defense of the Homeland), drypoint and etching, 1917, 22 x 16.

Figs. 76-79. From *Gestes de Femmes* (Chronicles of Women), dry-point and etching, 1917, 7 x 10.

77.

The earliest postwar etchings, the works which were sold by Galerie Georges Petit and eventually exported to the United States, were simple images—humorous, saucy portraits of beautiful girls, often seen in awkward predicaments. In *Le Masque Chinois*, 1919 (Fig. 81), the mask casts the lady with the cigarette a disapproving glance, while in *L'Ahurissement* (Bewilderment), 1920 (Fig. 82), the curious monkey tries to fit his mistress's shoe onto his own foot. These pictures are typical of many Icart etchings of this postwar period. His models were shapely, occasionally baring a breast or thigh, and entirely unconcerned with the embarrassment of their respective circumstances. In all these works, it is the personality of the female figure that is most important, not the dress or fashionable hat. *Les Oranges Renversées* (Spilled Oranges), 1921 (Fig. 83), is among the best of these early works. The lady is as sensual a harvester as one is likely to find in any orchard, and Icart mischievously sees to it that more than the oranges are spilling. The composition and graceful movement seen in this work are evidence of the talents that would continue to present themselves in his later efforts.

Les Chatons (Kittens), 1924 (Fig. 84), *Poupée Moderne* (French Doll), 1926 (Fig. 85), and *Le Bouddha Bleu* (The Blue Buddha), 1924 (Fig. 86), all employ props and animals to highlight the scene, but the emphasis is still on the beautiful woman, posed

79.

78.

individually or in groups, another trend that continued into later works.

The period 1919 to 1925 was one of great experimentation for Icart; his etchings during these years show a variety of graphic arts techniques. It was at this time that Icart discovered stippled grounds, feathering, *à la poupée,* and other etching methods. In 1931, he would write, with regard to all he had learned about drypoint, "But it must be remembered that etching is a science, and like all science it is only by constant practice and time that perfection can be achieved. I engraved my first drypoint twenty years ago, and I learn something new with each of my plates. This is said merely as a reminder to all artists that the more advancement that is made in art the wider extend the boundaries for possible perfection." [42]

After his journey to the United States in 1922, Icart, taken with the vitality of the American people, offered them works that often became more personal. *En Auto* (Motoring), 1923 (Fig. 87), features Fanny and her dog Dollar in Icart's automobile. *Avant le Raid,* 1925 (Fig. 37), recalled a heroic moment of World War I. Certainly his most fertile creative period began after the trip to the United States, when Icart produced several hundred etchings for the blossoming American market.

Fig. 80. *Dans les Tranchées* (In the Trenches), drypoint and etching, 1918, 18½ x 11½.

Fig. 81. *Le Masque Chinoise* (Chinese Mask), drypoint and etching, 1919.

Fig. 82. *L'Ahurissement* (Bewilderment), drypoint and etching, 1920, 20 x 25.

Fig. 83. *Les Oranges Renversées* (Spilled Oranges), drypoint and etching, 1921.

Fig. 84. *Les Chatons* (Kittens), drypoint and etching, 1924.

Fig. 85. *Poupée Moderne* (French Doll), drypoint and etching, 1926, 18 x 14.

Fig. 86. *Le Bouddha Bleu* (The Blue Buddha), drypoint and etching, 1924, 19 x 13½.

Fig. 87. *En Auto* (Motoring), drypoint and etching, 1923, 18½ x 14.

Fig. 88. *Méditation* (Golden Veil), drypoint and etching, 1930, 20 x 15.

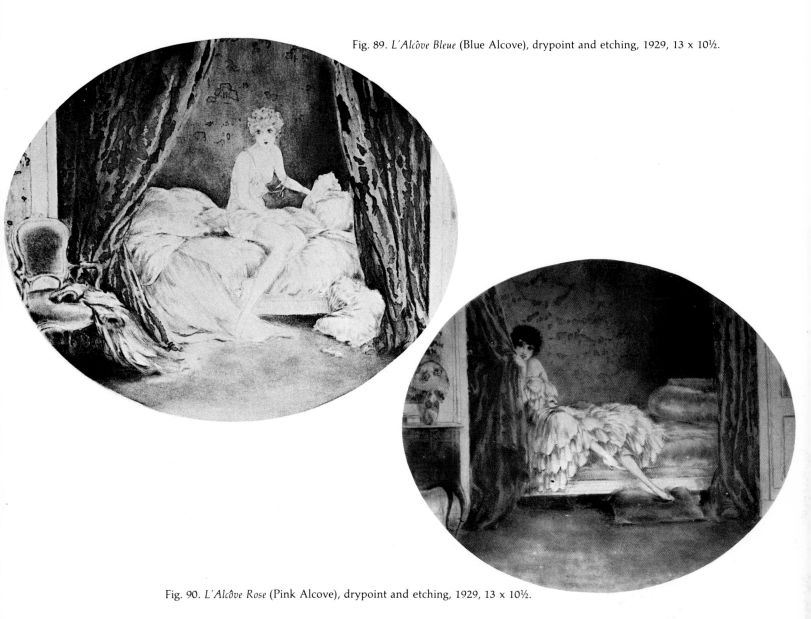

Fig. 89. *L'Alcôve Bleue* (Blue Alcove), drypoint and etching, 1929, 13 x 10½.

Fig. 90. *L'Alcôve Rose* (Pink Alcove), drypoint and etching, 1929, 13 x 10½.

While some works were, of course, more successful than others, both as artistic expressions and as commercial products, the two factors did not always blend. *Hortensias*, 1929 (Fig. 25), the most popular Icart etching ever created, is awkwardly posed and an artistic failure. Still, it epitomizes the "bedroom picture," a genre that Icart introduced to the American market. No doubt inspired by Fanny's moods or poses, Icart created dozens of pictures which displayed delicate eroticism in an elegant setting of cushions or flowers.

Méditation (Golden Veil), 1930 (Fig. 88), is among the most successful of Icart's "bedroom pictures." Delicately drawn, employing a range of colors, the etching has a blatant suggestiveness. The brilliant use of a gold lace motif on Fanny's body, her "come hither" look, even the long red cigarette holder, make it one of Icart's most amusing and erotic pieces. Equally erotic, though less obvious in their sensuality, are *L'Alcôve Bleue*, 1929 (Fig. 89), and *L'Alcôve Rose*, 1929 (Fig. 90). Occasionally, Icart would employ the boudoir as a setting for heroines of literature or fairy tales. *La Belle au Bois Dormant* (Sleeping Beauty), 1927 (Fig. 91), does fair justice to the perspective in the work. Icart's *Thaïs*, 1927 (Fig. 92), as in the notorious painting of the same name, modeled after Claudia Victrix, is as provocative as any Egyptian lady has a right to be. The use of cheetahs in the composition exemplifies Icart's frequent use of animals to highlight such exotic portraits.

A work in which an animal takes equal prominence with the woman is *Les Yeux* (Two Beauties), 1931 (Fig. 93). Originally inspired by a snapshot of Fanny and Dollar in the grass at Itteville, it is a captivating work. The small menagerie of dogs, cats, and other pets that the Icarts kept at Itteville inspired many etchings, among them *Chien et Chat* (Dear Friends), 1929 (Fig. 94), and *Enigme* (Sweet Mystery), 1935 (Fig. 95), casual and formal portraits, respectively, of Fanny with her pets.

While American buyers found such scenes appealing, Icart also supplied the graphics trade with etchings that reflected less personal themes, such as those works featuring operatic heroines. Among the ladies of music he etched were Carmen, seen in *Séville*, 1928 (Fig. 96); Tosca of Puccini's opera of the same name, 1928 (Fig. 97); and *Faust*, 1928 (Fig. 98), which features the beautiful Marguerite, heroine of the operas by Berlioz (1846), Gounod (1859), and Boïto (1868).

Icart created a number of etchings of heroines from life and from literature, including Sappho, 1929, Madame Bovary, 1929, and Mimi Pinson, 1927 (seen on the dust jacket of this volume). Icart's literary tastes also sparked the creation of works depicting male characters. *Casanova*, 1928 (Fig. 99), *D'Artagnan* of Dumas's *The Three*

Fig. 91. *La Belle au Bois Dormant* (Sleeping Beauty), drypoint and etching, 1927, 19½ x 15½.

Figures 92–93 appear on page 78.

Musketeers, 1931 (Fig. 100), and *Des Grieux* (The Lovers) of Abbé Prévost's *Manon Lescaut*, 1930 (Fig. 101), as well as others, were privileged to appear in Icart etchings, and always in the company of a beautiful woman.

Surprisingly, those Icart etchings which had the most limited appeal in the United States were the nudes. With the exception of such dramatic pieces as *Grande Eve* (Eve and the Serpent), 1934 (Fig. 20), Icart's nudes were not quite the erotic fare one would expect. Playfulness, luxury—in short, a spirit of good, clean fun—is all one finds in most of his *femmes nues*. American buyers seemed to respond more favorably to the implied sensuality of the Icart models who lay on fat pillows in their negligées than they did to the obvious nakedness exhibited in such works as *Fumée* (Smoke), 1926 (Fig. 102), *Masque Noir* (Masked), 1933 (Fig. 103), and *Paravent de Lacque* (Unmasked), 1933 (Fig. 104). Since the nudes were not big sellers at the time of their creation, they were printed in limited quantities, leaving today's collectors few impressions from which to choose. *Sommeil* (Repose), 1933 (Fig. 105), a four-foot long work, was so huge that displaying it presented an obvious problem, and, hence, few buyers could be found. It was therefore limited to an edition of only one hundred impressions.

Fig. 94. *Chien et Chat* (Dear Friends), drypoint and etching, 1929.

Fig. 95. *Enigme* (Sweet Mystery), drypoint and etching, 1935, 16 x 20½.

Fig. 92. *Thaïs*, drypoint and etching, 1927, 20 x 16.

Fig. 93. *Les Yeux* (Two Beauties), drypoint and etching, 1931, 24 x 17.

Fig. 96. *Séville*, drypoint and etching, 1928, 13 x 20.

Fig. 97. *Tosca*, drypoint and etching, 1928, 13 x 21.

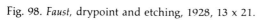

Fig. 98. *Faust*, drypoint and etching, 1928, 13 x 21.

Another work that had limited appeal was *Abat-jour* (Picnic), 1929, an unusual creation that was designed in the shape of a fan for possible use as a lampshade. While most Icart etchings were prepared in the rectangular or oval formats, *Abat-jour* illustrates the artist's willingness to experiment with a variety of shapes. In addition to the standard form, the artist also prepared etchings in a circular shape.

Among Icart's later etchings, the most creative are those that display his knack for fantasy. In *Papillon II* (Open Wings), 1936 (Fig. 106), and *Papillon III* (Woman in Wings), 1936 (Fig. 107), he adds new beauty to the butterfly by envisioning it as a young woman with brightly colored wings. *Léda,* 1934 (Fig. 109), one of the most sought after Icart etchings today, tells the tale of Leda and the Swan from Greek mythology, a theme that is repeated in Icart's oils, book illustrations, and watercolors. *Tabac Blond* (Illusion), 1940 (Fig. 108), shows a beautiful nude materializing in the smoke of a burning cigarette. It is a startling image, one that represents the very best of Louis Icart.

While the nudes were less popular than the boudoir scenes, Icart's greatest commercial successes were with the more traditional, humorous works, for example *Le Cocktail* (Martini), 1932 (Fig. 110), and *Au Bar* (Gay Trio), 1936 (Fig. 111). These works employ animals with humanized facial expressions for maximum decorative appeal, and their cuteness made them best sellers.

Probably the most atypical etchings the artist created were a series of aviation pieces during the early 1930s. *Le Souvenir* (The Memory), 1931 (Fig. 112), *L'Oiseau Blanc* (The White Bird), 1931 (Fig. 113), and *L'Oiseau dans la Tempête* (The Bird in the Storm), 1931 (Fig. 114), all honored famous French and American aviators. All are significant as much because of the absence of a female figure as for their historical value.

Le Souvenir recalls the flight of Captain Charles Nungesser and Captain François Coli, French war aces and pilots, who attempted a North Atlantic flight from Paris to New York on May 8, 1927, two weeks before Charles Lindbergh's famous transatlantic flight. Nungesser and Coli headed toward the sun in their plane, *White Bird,* from Paris's Le Bourget Field, but the plane disappeared within a few hours after takeoff. The Icart etchings, *Le Souvenir* and *L'Oiseau Blanc,* evoke the mysterious circumstances of the disappearance. In the first work, the wreath which floats on the water seems to emphasize the loneliness of the voyage. In the latter etching, a ravenous sea seems to reach up to pull the tiny plane into its depths. *L'Oiseau dans la Tempête,* commissioned by Rodman Wanamaker of the Wanamaker department stores in New York and Philadelphia, honors Admiral Richard E. Byrd, the aviator and polar explorer.

Icart rarely accepted commissions because such works were generally produced in small editions and were less profitable than works produced for a general market. Icart was, however, summoned by the Finnish Government to prepare a work which commemorated the invasion of Finland by Russia during the Russo-Finnish War, 1939–40. The artist accepted the commission because he abhorred such an invasion by a neighboring country into a smaller nation. His anger resulted in a striking work, *Finlande!,* 1940 (Fig. 115), which depicts a stricken female figure against the backdrop of the Finnish flag. In a state of semicrucifixion, she is drawn with blood pouring from her heart. A terrifying expression of the artist's indignation, the figure's rigid stance is atypical of many of the more "liquid" works Icart had etched previously, yet this absence of motion contributes to its power.

Indeed, Icart's ability to imbue his etchings with a sense of motion was perhaps his greatest talent. His use of sleek canines as in *L'Elan* (Zest), 1928 (Fig. 116), was one way of suggesting motion, and the use of long, sweeping strokes, especially evident in this etching, added greatly to the feeling of speed he wanted to achieve. In fact, the most popular Icart subject was the running *demoiselle* and her greyhounds in *Vitesse* (Speed), a work made into thousands of impressions, which had to be re-etched when the first copperplate wore out. The first version published in 1929 (Fig. 117), shows a gray dog running ahead of two black dogs and the young woman holding the leashes tightly to her breast. In the 1933 edition of the same work (Fig. 118), it is the black dog that runs ahead of the others, and the girl has no leash. Her right hand is instead placed on the collar of the dog nearest her. Icart never revealed why he felt these minor changes were necessary, although the second version of the etching may have been altered so as not to be confused with an unauthorized print of *Vitesse* being distributed at the time.

Racing dogs were not the only symbols of motion in Icart's etchings. *Yachting*, a colorful work done in 1936 (Fig. 119), uses the splashing sea and a precarious perspective to indicate motion. Motion is also the key element in *Joie de Vivre*, 1929 (Fig. 120), although it is more subtly employed. The etching features a girl with two dogs on a windy hilltop. The strong wind is an obvious element; the figure holds her hat tightly to her head and the dogs brace themselves stiffly against the force of the wind. *L'Averse* (Fig. 66) employs silhouetted background figures to indicate the force of the shower, but the drenched demoiselle in the foreground seems untroubled by her umbrellaless state. Her clothing and her position, however, indicate strong resistance to the driving rain and wind. *Pur-sang* (Fig. 48), is the epitome of action, though it is essentially a work of dual portraiture. It depicts Icart's daughter, Reine, on Rossinante, the white steed he bought after the production of *Don Quichotte de la Manche* was staged in Nice. Icart even achieves a sense of motion—or some would say imbalance—by the precarious packages carried by the cupid in *Les Colis* (Before Christmas), 1922 (Fig. 121), a work presented as a Christmas gift to friends during the year in which it was etched.

After the Second World War, Icart's etchings took on an increasingly impressionistic appearance, as did his paintings. At this time, Icart returned to etching on copper, but works like *Musique en Eté* (Summer Music), 1950 (Fig. 122), were unable to regenerate the following that had been lost in the United States during the war years. The newer works were almost exclusively aquatint, an attempt at adapting his oil painting techniques to the copperplate. Unfortunately, the later etchings had none of the cleverness, motion, or beauty of his earlier creations. Since the fashion for Icart's etchings had ended, not even the artist himself could find a formula for commercial success in the immediate postwar picture market. It was an austere time of unhappy memories for many millions, and Icart's flights of elegant fancy were ill suited to an era that was intent on repairing the emotional and physical damages of the war. Oddly enough, it would take three decades for his works to once again appear in the public consciousness, but today's collectors of Icart's etchings are as enthusiastic about his ebullient works as their predecessors were fifty years ago.

Rediscovering a forgotten artist, however, is not always an easy task. Since Icart had many imitators, today's admirers may have difficulty in recognizing and identifying Icart etchings. The etchings of Louis Icart, however, bear certain identifiable traits that, when known, easily prevent confusion with imitations and reproductions.

Because the original copperplates have been canceled or destroyed, the images are impossible to reproduce as etchings. A four-color reproduction will show the telltale screening so necessary to that form of reproductive work, and much of the vitality and color of the original will be lost in the process.

Fig. 99. *Casanova*, drypoint and etching, 1928, 14 x 21.

Fig. 100. *D'Artagnan*, drypoint and etching, 1931, 14 x 21.

Fig. 101. *Des Grieux* (The Lovers), drypoint and etching, 1930, 14 x 21.

Fig. 102. *Fumée* (Smoke), drypoint and etching, 1926, 20 x 15.

Fig. 103. *Masque Noir* (Masked), drypoint and etching, 1933, 8½ x 13.

Fig. 104. *Paravent de Lacque* (Unmasked), drypoint and etching, 1933, 8½ x 13.

Fig. 105. *Sommeil* (Repose), drypoint and etching, 1933, 45 x 19.

Fig. 107. *Papillon III* (Woman in Wings), drypoint and etching, 1936, 9 x 7.

Fig. 106. *Papillon II* (Open Wings), drypoint and etching, 1936, 9 x 7.

Fig. 108. *Tabac Blond* (Illusion), drypoint and etching, 1940, 9 x 19.

Fig. 109. *Léda*, drypoint and etching, 1934, 31 x 21.

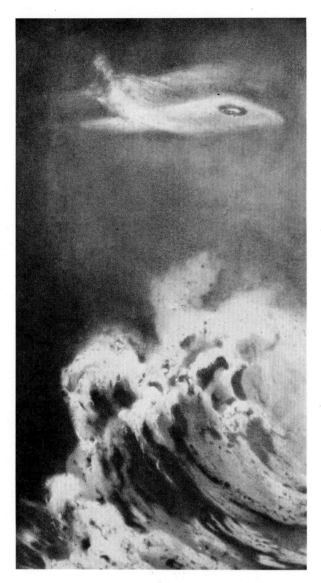

Fig. 113. *L'Oiseau Blanc* (The White Bird), drypoint and etching, 1931, 15 x 27. (The airplane in this etching may appear too streamlined for its time, but it appears so because the usual practice on such record flights was to drop the landing gear immediately after takeoff to help reduce weight and wind resistance. Specially prepared landing areas at the termination point of the journey allowed the planes to land safely on their bellies.)

Fig. 114. *L'Oiseau dans la Tempête* (The Bird in the Storm), drypoint and etching, 1931, 15 x 27.

Figures 110–112 appear on pages 90–91.

Fig. 115. *Finlande!*, drypoint and etching, 1940, 21 x 14.

Fig. 116. *L'Elan* (Zest), drypoint
and etching, 1928, 14 x 19.

Figures 117-119 appear on pages 94–95.

Fig. 110. *Le Cocktail* (Martini), drypoint and etching, 1932, 16½ x 12½.

Fig. 111. *Au Bar* (Gay Trio), drypoint and etching, 1936, 11½ x 19½.

Fig. 112. *Le Souvenir* (The Memory), drypoint and etching, 1931, 19½ x 16½.

Icart's etchings were also produced on the finest available papers, most commonly on Arches paper, a heavy stock that is still being used by artists today. Many Icart etchings, when held up to the light, show the watermarks of Arches, Van Gelder, or the other papers he used frequently. Some works have also been printed on Japanese Impérial paper, a stock which has a rice-paperlike translucence. In all cases, the artist attempted to adapt the paper stock to the subject at hand, blending all the elements of the art of etching as effectively as possible.

In the 1920s, when Icart's works became increasingly popular, he developed a small intaglio seal (Fig. 123) that was impressed into the corner of each etching destined for export to the United States. This seal was an additional guarantee of the originality of the work; it featured the windmill of the Moulin de la Galette (a famous Montmartre landmark) and the artist's initials.

Works registered with the U.S. Copyright Office in Washington, D.C., bear the impression of copyright notice along the top border. It must be remembered, however, that not all works bear this notice. Most etchings published before 1922, which had not been prepared for U.S. distribution, were not copyrighted; nor were etchings prepared solely for European distribution.

Another identification mark is *Gravure Garantie Originale*, which was rubber-stamped onto the farthest margin of the etching. Most Icart etchings were printed with ample margins of several inches which facilitated handling during the printing process. Most early works will show none of these features and bear only the pencil signature of the artist. As for the signature, it varies considerably from etching to etching, since a man's signature generally changes with time and shifting moods. Experienced collectors will take all these features into consideration before purchasing an Icart etching.

Fig. 120. *Joie de Vivre,* drypoint and etching, 1929, 15 x 23½.

Fig. 121. *Les Colis* (Before Christmas), drypoint and etching, circa 1922, 10 x 14.

Fig. 122. *Musique en Eté* (Summer Music), etching, 1950.

Fig. 117. *Vitesse* (Speed), drypoint and etching, 1929, 25 x 15½.

Fig. 118. *Vitesse* (Speed), proof copy, 1933, 25 x 15½.

Fig. 119. *Yachting*, drypoint and etching, 1936, 24½ x 19.

Identification and authentication of Icart etchings have proved to be less of a problem than locating desired pieces. The supply of etchings that are popular with today's admirers is understandably limited and, as art collectors become aware of the works of this forgotten genius, the demand naturally increases. Regrettably, admirers must make do with the current supplies of Icart etchings since there will be no more etchings printed on demand from American galleries.

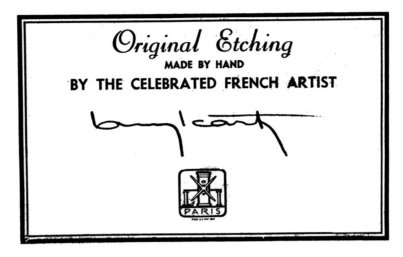

Fig. 123. An example of the paper label which accompanied many Icart etchings exported to the United States. It shows the windmill chop mark that Icart impressed into the corners of etchings intended for U.S. distribution.

CHAPTER 3

Fig. 126. *Amsterdam,* oil, 1921, 19½ x 24. On the reverse side of this canvas, Icart wrote, "For Fanny, a souvenir of our wonderful trip."

MASTER OF THE GOLDEN PALETTE

ONE LOOK AT ICART'S PROVOCATIVE OIL PAINTING *Enigme* (SWEET MYSTERY), 1922 (FIG. 124), and one can easily understand why his early oils earned him the name "master of the golden palette." Deep, fiery reds and golds dominated his works. Unlike the etchings, which were designed to appeal to a specific market, Icart's early oils were the synthesis of his talent and self-expression. The artist had been so impressed with the beauty of Italy, that many of his paintings from 1918 to 1925 concentrated on capturing the golden landscapes of that land. Icart called this phase of his oil painting career *manière rouge,* and the style is typified by *L'Invitation,* 1920 (Fig. 125). This work, set in Venice, repeats an eighteenth-century theme: a lean, satanic masquerader who tempts a waiflike innocent to join him in a mysterious gondola. The viewer can only guess at her answer, and, if she consents, at the eventual destination, but this mystery is part of the charm and haunting beauty of this work.

In a March 1920 review of Icart canvases exhibited at the Galerie Simonson in Paris, *Le Matin,* the Paris daily, noted: "Granada, Venice, Versailles, and some sensual bedroom intimacies. Nights of moonlight on the water, days of fruits and flowers and foliage. Ample translucence molds the bodies, where the blood courses in abundance. Mythological satyrs stand near the eternal woman, with their eternal desires. This is

Figures 124–125 appear on pages 98–99.

Fig. 124. *Enigme* (Sweet Mystery), oil, 1922, 22½ x 29.

the world we find here, a world that Icart has presented us with his prestigious brush." [43]

Not all the critics, however, had nice things to say about Icart's golden palette. A visiting critic from the *London Daily Mail* called the paintings "lurid pictures," [44] while another critic from the Paris *L'Oeuvre* said, "Venetian tinsel, parks and fauns, the sentimental effects of a disciple of LaTouche, a puerile business. This foolishness merits a burst of laughter." [45]

Icart was unaffected by reviews. "In painting," he said, "the public is the only judge." [46] Above all, Icart believed in the strength of personal taste, and the critics were too small a segment of the population to matter very much. Icart's views on evaluating and purchasing a work of art are as applicable today as they were when he first expressed them in 1923:

> One should consider the two values of a canvas, not only the speculative potential and the important signature, but also how well the painting rejuvenates the spirit. If it succeeds in this way, then the painting is necessarily good, which is when it satisfies the artist . . . for I persist in saying that it is not necessary to be a connoisseur to make a good acquisition. Ignore the signature. If the work pleases the eye at the same time that it enchants the spirit and incites the reverie, it is for the good. The money invested will repay itself, for something that touches one soul will surely capture another. [47]

Just as Paolo Veronese, Jean Honoré Fragonard, and Jean Antoine Watteau had captured his soul with their subjects and style, Icart attempted to touch others with his own treatment of the same themes. Icart found, in the works of a later generation of painters—Claude Monet, Edgar Degas, and Auguste Renoir—the oil painting techniques that suited him best. At first glance, the fiery tones of the *manière rouge* period seem to be a variation on Fauvist techniques, but a studied analysis reveals Icart's roots to be firmly embedded in the soil of Impressionism. The artist's *Amsterdam, 1921* (Fig. 126), for example, is typical of his early Impressionism. The muted tones and subtle brushwork give this cityscape the same translucence that made his Venetian scenes such sources of fantasy. An early portrait of *Fanny and Reine, 1925* (Fig. 127), however,

Fig. 125. *L'Invitation*, oil, 1920, 19½ x 24.

99

Fig. 127. *Fanny and Reine,* oil, 1925, 25½ x 36.

abandons the *manière rouge* in favor of the more subtle colors reminiscent of Renoir. Icart did not attempt to copy any style or work from its original creator, but rather to apply Impressionist techniques to his own vision.

"I cannot refrain from kneeling before Watteau," he stated, "and before the Impressionists, as well as before the first, and the greatest of them all: Paolo Cagliari, le Veronese. These have been my only teachers. In Veronese my eyes attempt to capture the difficult secret of his golden tones, of his silky and shifting colors." [48]

But while Icart spoke often of influences from the schools, he also considered himself an Impressionist. His brush techniques owed much to that school, even though his use of color was closer to the frescoes he had seen in the chapels and museums of Italy. Icart's early palette was rich in blends of red, green, and yellow, in deep tones fitting the luxurious fancies of his imagination. The golds were reserved for the skin of his elegant beauties, and all around them, he applied his paints thickly. His portrait of Fanny, *Joie de Vivre,* 1923 (Fig. 128), shows effective use of this early method of coloring. *Coursing,* 1920 (Fig. 129), combines the Icart palette with a sense of speed that was beginning to popularize his etchings. This painting was one of several variations, since *Coursing* was later seen in other paintings and etchings. In addition to the bold feeling of movement and freedom, the work signified one of his first attempts to employ animals as important features of a canvas. Icart, in fact, remarked at the time the work was exhibited, ". . . I am a disciple of feminine beauty, not only the beauty of her nature, but of her physical beauty as well. It is for this reason that in my recent works I have introduced greyhounds and borzois. They are the perfect complement to the graceful lines of the feminine form." [49]

Icart's oil paintings were usually completed in one sitting. His characteristic short brush stroke infused them with a feeling of spontaneity. Appearing to have been created with complete abandon, the works were actually carefully considered

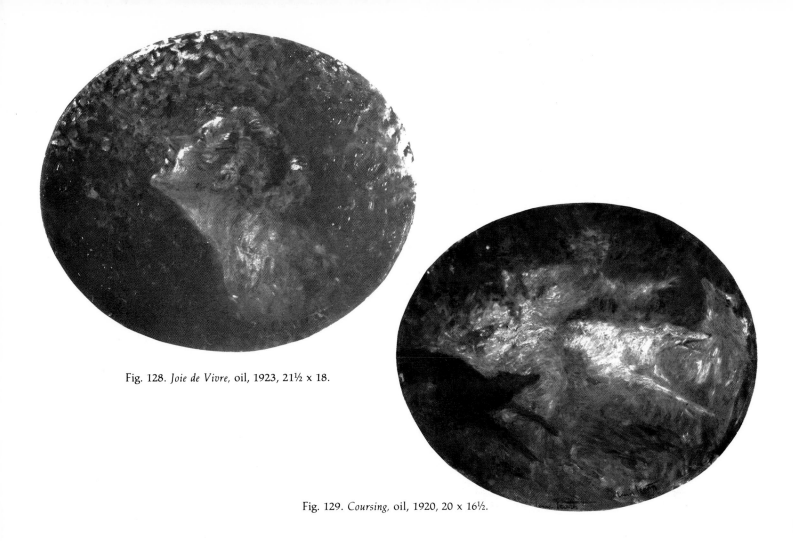

Fig. 128. *Joie de Vivre*, oil, 1923, 21½ x 18.

Fig. 129. *Coursing*, oil, 1920, 20 x 16½.

experiments in the use of color and stroke. Icart often deliberated for days over the composition and tonal qualities of a work before placing brush to canvas; the act of painting to Icart required careful contemplation and then a spontaneous attack.

"A painting cannot be a colored photograph," he said. "When you are before a canvas, the subject must be treated in such a fashion that your thoughts spring forth. It must be born of a dream or an impression. It must be a departure to a land of fancy." [50]

In the United States, Louis Icart was little known as an oil painter. His early canvases, although seen regularly in Paris galleries, were exhibited here infrequently. While a few oils were kept on display at the Louis Icart Society showroom at 10 West 33rd Street in New York City, the Icart oils had only three major American showings: in 1922, when the artist visited America for the first time; in 1932, when the Louis Icart Society introduced the new series of oils called *"les visions blanches"*; and in 1948, when Icart returned to the United States in a vain attempt to revive interest in his work.

Icart's first organized American expositions were held in December 1922 and January 1923, at the Wanamaker department store art galleries, the first in New York City, the second in Philadelphia. Icart was present at the exhibits to promote his etchings and to determine the direction of future works for the American market. The Wanamaker exhibits featured over forty oil paintings, yet they were sadly outnumbered and overshadowed by his etchings, drawings, and fashion sketches. These pieces were more appealing to American buyers; their vitality and humor seemed more vigorous, more entertaining than that of the paintings. Being mysterious and demanding study, the oils failed to evoke the same feelings. And 1922—in the era of the speakeasy and the flapper—was no year to ask Americans to consider anything seriously.

Fig. 130. *Eve*, oil, 1934.

During his visit to the United States, however, Icart had ample opportunity to paint, and many afternoons were spent in capturing the architectural marvels of New York City. New York Harbor, the Flatiron Building, the Sixth Avenue "El" trains, Wall Street, all became his subjects. As he had done with the scenes of Venice, Icart rendered New York a cityscape of powerful structures and shadows bathed in the red light of sunset.

Upon his return to France, Icart, not having the heart to deny his American following the etchings they demanded (nor the will to forgo the luxury their dollars provided), increased his production of copperplate etchings and thus painted infrequently. The artist still accepted portrait commissions, usually to paint prominent actresses and other ladies of high society, but his favorite model for oils, as for etchings, was always Fanny. In spite of the pressures to create etchings for the American market, Icart managed to immortalize her in over one hundred canvases.

Icart continued to develop his oil painting techniques when he found the time. As his work progressed, he was no longer limited to a palette of red and gold, and he concentrated more on stroke, often shifting away from the bold, expressive colors he had once favored. Certain subjects demanded a soft tone that could never be achieved with the bright colors he had previously favored. As his early colors seemed to come from the earth, his later colors came from the heavens. Icart incorporated his new color scheme more often in the 1930s, and it is at its most successful in *Carnaval*, 1932 (Fig. 131), a masterpiece of composition, coloring, and movement. This graceful work, which embodies an oft-repeated theme of the artist, pictures the clown as a lover, embracing his lady in a frenzied passion. *Eve*, 1934 (Fig. 130), is a charming expression of lost innocence, a beautiful woman who is enhanced by the pastel tones of Icart's brush.

This work was part of the series of canvases called *les visions blanches* which was shipped to New York in the fall of 1932 for display at the Metropolitan Galleries. *Art Digest* termed the works "decorative white visions," [51] but little attention was paid to the exhibit in the American press. Without the presence of the colorful Frenchman and his beautiful wife, the paintings did not cause a stir.

Many of the characteristics found in Icart's etchings of the 1920s and 1930s were echoed by the new oils. *Dame aux Camélias, Hortensias, Joie de Vivre,* and other subjects that had been seen as etchings reappeared in *les visions blanches* and, in later years, Icart painted numerous still lifes (Fig. 132).

The unlikely pose of Icart's *Eve in Paradise*, 1934 (Fig. 133), is both erotic and amusing. Similarly Icart interpreted the legend of Leda and the Swan, this time in oil, 1937 (Fig. 134). The painting, however, shows more obvious sexuality and more humor than the etching.

Such fantasies in oil were in keeping with Icart's carefree, luxurious lifestyle, but on June 11, 1940, with the German invasion of France, the artist turned his attentions to a different kind of oil painting, a style that was both documentary and emotional.

With great sorrow, the artist read reports of his countrymen fleeing their homes in the North, descending on Paris by the thousands. But the city had shut itself up like a frightened, immobile turtle to await the invaders.

News of the Exodus prompted Icart to develop on another level. Leaving his home to join the multitudes of fleeing countrymen from the North, he shared the miseries of their route for three days and nights. He thus primed himself well for an important new series of paintings, *L'Exode*, fifty striking oils that document the horrors of the flight from the Germans.

Fig. 131. *Carnaval*, oil, 1932, 52 x 64.

Fig. 132. *Lilas et Roses*, still life, oil, circa 1930, 34½ x 51.

Fig. 133. *Eve in Paradise*, oil, circa 1934.

Fig. 134. *Léda*, oil, circa 1937, 51 x 38.

Icart's *L'Exode* did not concern itself so much with technique as with the need to express the realities of those agonizing days. The paintings are in tones of green and brown, and they exhibit the characteristic rapid brushstroke of Icart, a feature which adds greatly to their power. The paintings have the compelling objectivity of news photos. In Figure 135, the oppressive shadow of a German plane hangs ominously over a multitude of escapees as they pass the weapons of war. Figures 136 to 138 show terror on their faces as they run from the unseen enemy, and, at the same time, reveal how the fleeing civilian population hampered the movement of French troops and weapons, a situation which indirectly helped the German invaders.

Icart was never permitted to display his *L'Exode* series in an occupied Paris. It is an aspect of his career that sadly missed recognition.

After the liberation of Paris, Icart was too occupied with finding ways to reconstruct his popularity in America to exhibit the works from *L'Exode*, and they were stored away until their recent rediscovery.

During the Occupation, much of the artist's time was spent in painting the fanciful, "pretty" pictures that became a trademark of his later years as a painter. This new series of oils was yet a further synthesis of *fêtes galantes*, clever continuations of his earlier experiments with a limited palette of blues, grays, and whites. In these new works, Icart's Impressionism came into full blossom.

Certainly they shared the romanticism of the *manière rouge* pieces, but gone was the whimsical imagination of cities bathed in golden dew and forests ablaze with autumn colors. Icart found contentment in painting the real-life fairy gardens of Paris—*Place Vendôme, Place du Tertre, the Tuileries*. His models were young women of the city, a graceful gathering of summer dresses and parasols. In the beauty and wonder of the Frenchwoman, Icart found a wealth of romance that exceeded any he had observed before. *Fanny*, 1942 (Fig. 139), and *Fanny and Chou-Chou*, 1943 (Fig. 140), show why the artist's new palette earned him his continued reputation as a painter of feminine grace.

Icart once said, "It has been said that they are too lovely. But is the beauty of a woman in a painting somehow different from the natural beauty of a woman? Surely my models . . . have grace, and this alone is eternal." [52]

Many of Icart's *visions blanches* oils were highly experimental, almost abstract in their approach, as in *Petits Chats* (Kittens), circa 1945 (Fig. 141). Most, however, were soft, sensitive, pastel portraits or scenes. Many works, such as *Dans les Rêves* (Meditation), 1932 (Fig. 142), and various portraits of Fanny, such as *Fanny and Bib* 1940 (Fig. 143), were as graceful in *les visions blanches* as they had been in the reds and golds of *manière rouge*. His childhood friend, Jules Esquirol, on visiting the Icart home in 1945, just after the war, made the following observations on the new series of canvases:

> His studio was a symphony in white . . . from top to bottom . . . the woman, the modern woman, a song under his paintbrush . . . the purity of her form, the grace of her body, the lure of her sex, the elegance of her attire.
>
> Greuze, Lancret, Mignard?
>
> Perhaps, but on another plane, with more mystery, dreaminess, transparency, and love.
>
> One bathed in an atmosphere of grace.
>
> The perfumes of spring enveloped one.
>
> "Well," asked Icart.
>
> I embraced him as a response.
>
> How can one class this artist, and where can one class him?

Let us remember that he had never cleared the threshold of l'École des Beaux
Arts, the door of a studio, the entranceway of any Academy.
And this here, hard to believe, is rigorously true.
He did it alone.
He never "visited" with his colleagues.
He never took the responsibility of a tutelage upon himself.
He is Icart.
That is enough.
He has touched the spirit of his colleagues, a divination which sparks of the
supernatural. Poet, he could make poems with his palette.[53]

When Icart came to the United States with a group of paintings from *les visions
blanches* in December 1948, for a special exhibit at the New York Graphic Society
galleries, critics viewed the works as decorative accessories, not as works of art in their
own right. Too much of the artist's past, too great a portion of his artistry had been
kept from the Americans, who were unable to base their responses to his work on his
total output. The kindest comments came from a visiting Los Angeles critic who wrote,
"The women painted by Icart seem to wait for Don Juan, their eyes lost in a dream, the
dream which is most dear to them—love. This is why Icart goes right to the heart. In all
of his paintings, whether of one woman or several women . . . it is always potentially
the same figure, the spirit of love." [54]

Though the response in America was lukewarm, Icart still looked forward to
many years of exploration in oil. He often spoke of his life as a clipper ship in full sail,
exploring uncharted seas, delving into new worlds. For his wife, Icart painted just such
a ship, *Le Voyage*, 1945 (Fig. 144), a vessel born of his dreams, and he christened its
maiden voyage on canvas with a thoughtful poem:

> *To sail away . . . this is the voyage . . .*
> *It is to search elsewhere for other faces, for other*
> *flowers, for other nests, for other songs,*
> *other skies.*
> *It is to always recede from the radiant horizon . . .*
> *It is a wish to breathe all the exotic perfumes . . .*
> *A wish to float through the night on the Ganges, the*
> *Danube, the Nile, or the fiery Bosphorus.*
> *It is the desire for a new red, or a new blue.*
> *It is to leave the daily chains behind you.*
> *It is a wish to escape from a place of toil,*
> *Through the hidden lands behind the summits, those*
> *lands which perhaps you will never reach. . . .*[55]

LOUIS ICART

The poet, like the painter, was unable to reach many of those lands. Icart's sudden
death in 1950 came as he was ascending into a new realm of creativity, one that might
have brought him the recognition he deserved as a painter.

Figs. 135-138. From *L'Exode* (Exodus), oil, 1940, 24 x 20.

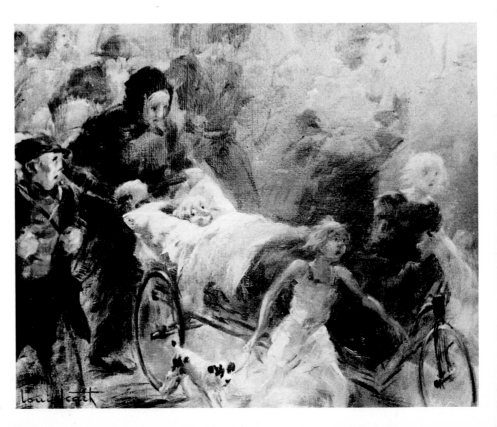

136.

137.

138.

Fig. 139. *Fanny*, oil, 1942.

Fig. 141. *Petits Chats* (Kittens), oil, circa 1945.

Fig. 140. *Fanny and Chou-Chou*, oil, 1943.

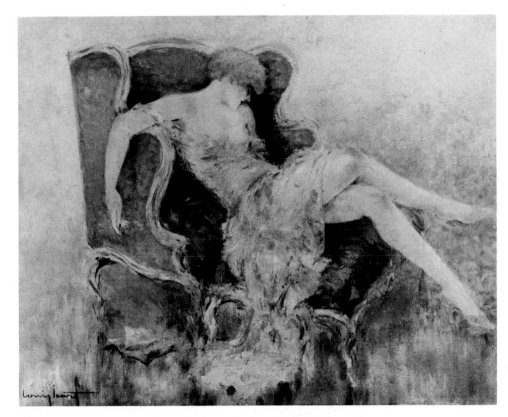

Fig. 142. *Dans les Rêves* (Meditation), oil, 1932, 38 x 51.

Fig. 143. *Fanny and Bibi*, oil, 1940, 25½ x 32.

Fig. 144. *Le Voyage*, oil, 1945, 38 x 51.

CHAPTER 4

DREAMS IN WATERCOLOR

Fig. 145. *Joie de Vivre*, watercolor, 1933, 9 x 12.

LOUIS ICART'S WATERCOLORS ARE HIS RAREST WORKS. A PROLIFIC GRAPHIC ARTIST AND OIL painter, he had little time for watercolor, a medium he used only occasionally to make a quick color sketch or to highlight a pencil drawing. Ironically, the artist showed his greatest potential for brilliance with the watercolor brush. His skill with the medium, however, was unknown except to a small group of friends and admirers.

Joie de Vivre (Fig. 145) is a watercolor portraying a typical Icart scene: the graceful form of female beauty with a sleek canine in a brisk wind. The light use of color and the quick line recall some of the aquatints he did for his *livres d'artiste.*

But there is another side to Icart the watercolorist—one occasionally seen in the more mysterious books he illustrated. In fact, it was one of the lithographic illustrations for *Les Fleurs du Mal* that inspired a series of twenty-four watercolors, executed around 1945, based on the Baudelaire poems. These works are without a doubt the artist's best work in this medium, and they rank with his finest creations in other mediums.

Le Léthé (Fig. 146), *Les Phares* (Fig. 147), and *Le Chat* (Fig. 148) are sensitive works that employ the watercolor brush as if it were in the hands of symbolists Gustave

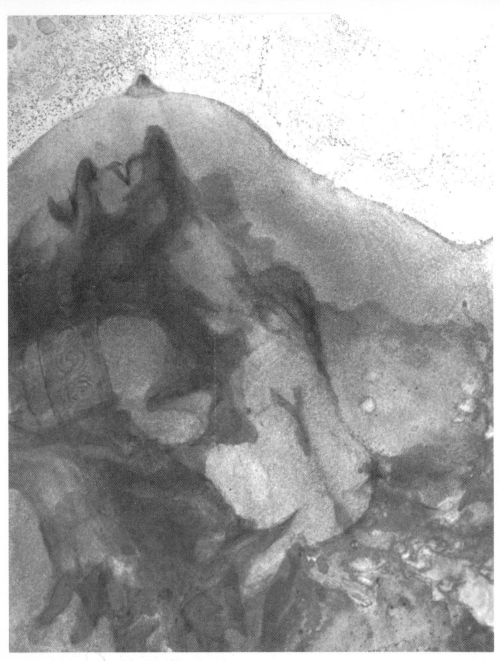

Fig. 146. *Le Léthé*, watercolor for *Les Fleurs du Mal*, circa 1945, 9 x 12.

Moreau (1826–98) or Odilon Redon (1840–1916). Icart's backgrounds are created with a watercolor wash that seems to sparkle like a jeweled veil. The works are rich in muted images; they are dreamlike; within their borders they present the varied imaginings of Baudelaire's poems. The penetrating figure in *Le Chat* is Baudelaire himself, set against a backdrop of multicolored shadows and veiled foregrounds. *La Beauté* (Fig. 149) is again reminiscent of many portraits of Fanny, while *Abel et Cain* (Fig. 150) evokes nightmarish images of treachery and death. Similarly, *Le Voyage* (Fig. 151) is a descent into the world of death, seen by Icart in a terrifying blend of browns and blacks.

The watercolors adapt many of the techniques which Icart used regularly in his etching work. The use of spots of varying colors to create a veiled effect in *Les Bijoux* (Fig. 152) is similar to the effect created with stippled ground. Equally striking are the sudden, unexpected reds and blues that seem so incongruous, yet which blend so well to create the total effect of the work. Similarly, the translucent washes join together to aid in evoking the subtle nuances of Baudelaire's poetry.

Les Fleurs du Mal obviously held great meaning for Louis Icart, and he responded by creating a magnificent counterpart to them. Expressions of genius, they represent the culmination of years of experimentation.

Figures 147–148 appear on page 118.

Fig. 149. *La Beauté,* watercolor for *Les Fleurs du Mal,* circa 1945, 9 x 12.

Fig. 147. *Les Phares,* watercolor for *Les Fleurs du Mal,*
circa 1945, 9 × 12.

Fig. 148. *Le Chat,* watercolor for *Les Fleurs du Mal,* circa 1945, 9 × 12.

Figures 150–151 appear on page 120.

Fig. 152. *Les Bijoux*, watercolor for *Les Fleurs du Mal*, circa 1945, 9 x 12.

Fig. 150. *Abel et Cain*, watercolor for *Les Fleurs du Mal*, circa 1945, 9 x 12.

Fig. 151. *Le Voyage*, watercolor for *Les Fleurs du Mal*, circa 1945, 9 x 12.

CHAPTER 5

LOUIS
ICART
AND THE
LIVRE
D'ARTISTE

Fig. 153. From *L'Ingénue Libertine,* drypoint and etching, 1926.

To UNDERSTAND LOUIS ICART'S ROLE AS AN ILLUSTRATOR OF FINE BOOKS, IT IS IMPORTANT TO examine the history and prominence of the *livre d'artiste* within the framework of French contemporary arts.

Virtually unknown outside of France, the *livre d'artiste*—alternately called *livre de peintre, beau livre* and *édition de luxe*—represents the quintessence of fine book publishing.

Speaking literally, *livre d'artiste* translates as "artist's book," and a more fitting definition would be difficult to apply. An aesthetically successful *livre d'artiste* is a work of art, born of the combined talents of printer and graphic artist. At the core of the *livre d'artiste* are original illustrations by a painter, sculptor, or graphic artist, who is known as a *peintre-graveur*. The illustrations are invariably produced by some autographic artistic process such as lithography, etching, aquatint, or woodcut, and the volumes are therefore necessarily limited to a small printing, usually 1,000 copies or fewer, with most editions averaging in the 300-copy range.

Because of the expense of binding such limited editions, most *livres d'artistes* are issued *en feuilles* or unbound, and are boxed in slipcases. Nearly every aspect of the *livre d'artiste* is observed and approved by the *peintre-graveur*. The typefaces, slipcase design, illumination, and other features of the completed project are created either by the artist or by fine typographers in consultation with him. Icart, who worked with many master printers, was often considered the *maître d'oeuvre*, responsible for the co-ordination and final outcome of the entire work, though in most cases he provided only the illustrations.

During the artist's lifetime, the audience for the *livre d'artiste* consisted almost exclusively of societies of collectors (not unlike the book clubs we know today), which gathered together to commission illustrated volumes of important literary works. Artists and printers worked out of varous French ateliers, and often the text and illustrations were printed in separate locations.

Depending on the fame and status of the artist selected to illustrate the works, the books cost up to several hundred dollars each. Icart was certainly in distinguished company in his role as a *peintre-graveur;* among other artists who illustrated *livres d'artistes* are Henri de Toulouse-Lautrec, Auguste Rodin, Georges Rouault, Raoul Dufy, Alberto Giacometti, Jean Cocteau, and Marcel Vertés. Pablo Picasso, who was never known for lack of creative energy, supplied the art world with dozens of *livres d'artistes.*

The *livre d'artiste* evolved into its twentieth-century format in 1900 after the publication of Verlaine's *Parallèlement,* which featured lithographic illustrations by Pierre Bonnard. The artist was commissioned to illustrate the book by Ambroise Vollard, a progressive publisher and art dealer, who saw the photomechanical age of printing approaching rapidly and sensed its threat to fine bookmaking. Without Vollard's support of artists and encouragement of the *livre d'artiste* concept, bookmaking as an art form could easily have been a victim of the powerful forces of profit and mass production. Vollard realized that no halftone could ever achieve the subtle effects and artistry inherent in an original lithograph or etching. He also knew that large publishing houses could not afford to print their books on handmade papers, with hand-set type, or give them other attributes of exclusivity.

Each *livre d'artiste* is its own complex series of parts, generally outlined in the *justification du tirage* or *achevé d'imprimer,* which correspond to the colophon found in some English and American books. Because *livres d'artistes* are generally printed on hand-operated presses, the completed edition of a book is often divided into several states in which the first numbers of the edition are more valuable than the later numbers.

For example, in an edition of 200, works numbered one to ten might be printed on special paper such as *Japon Super Nacré* and might include one or more extra sets of illustrations. In some cases, when the illustraions are produced as etchings, early numbers might include one or more original copperplates, which have been inked and permanently gilded. Not only does this addition make the early numbers of the book more sought after but this distribution of the original plates prevents duplication of the completed sets of illustrations.

As do many artists today, Icart would sometimes add *remarques* or *croquis* to the bottom margins of plates in early numbers of his editions. In some books, the artist included an original sketch or drawing. The value of a volume may merely be determined by the artist's pencil signature on the title page. Icart, who was especially parsimonious with his signature in the *livre d'artiste,* signed few books. In most cases, the *justification du tirage* indicates which volumes are signed and where the signatures may be found.

The artist is not always the major artistic contributor to the *livre d'artiste.* The printers' *ateliers* may contribute illumination, marginal decorations, or even a new typeface design, a feature reserved only for the most exclusive editions.

Even the types of paper used are an important consideration. Vellum, woven paper made from pure rag such as *Vélin de Rives* or *Vélin d'Arches*, are smooth papers which adapt readily to most forms of graphic impression and are therefore seen most often in the *livre d'artiste*. *Japon Nacré* and *Papier de Chine* are delicate papers which are especially useful for fine typefaces and the thin lines of copperplate etchings. On the other hand, the rough surfaced *Auvergne* papers are best suited to lithographs and large typefaces. Icart often used several papers within an edition to further accent the exclusivity of earlier numbers.

Icart was attracted to the *livre d'artiste* for several reasons: primarily, because he viewed bookmaking as another art form to be explored and mastered. Additionally, because of the *livre d'artiste*'s limited and exclusive audience, he was able to enter the world of erotic art. In the *livre d'artiste* Icart could give unrestricted expression, and freely display erotic creations that were unacceptable in his etchings and paintings. The buyers of *livres d'artistes* indeed welcomed the erotic content, and they responded gratefully to artists who believed, as they did, that illustrations for Baudelaire, Rabelais, and other greats of French literature should be as uninhibited as their source material.

Just as Icart's oil paintings show significant stylistic variations during different periods of his career, so are these differences reflected in his book illustrations. The artist approached each work from a different viewpoint, selecting the style and artistic medium he felt best suited the nature of the author's work. Icart's book illustrations are done in several media—lithography, monotype, etching, aquatint, and watercolor. The artist's preference, of course, was etching, and the greater part of his *livre d'artiste* output employs this form.

Form, however, was not the only difference. Some of the stylistic changes among the various creations are so pronounced that the untrained observer could readily assume they were executed by different artists. Yet the disparity in styles is not so great that certain of Icart's trademarks cannot be distinguished. The artist's excellent sense of composition and movement, his humor, and, as always, the graceful female subjects are generally recognizable. In some works, Icart includes other elements—a distinct sense of characterization, strong eroticism, and a precise ability to blend the mood of the artwork with the flavor of the text. Once given the subject matter, Icart molded his creations to the forms demanded by the authors, and a more alluring and compatible partnership would be hard to find. His illustrations for *Dame aux Camélias*, for example, are as gentle as the tender love affair between Marguerite Gautier and Armand Duval. His works for *Les Fleurs du Mal* and *Le Sixième Mariage de Barbe-Bleue* are rich in ominous textures and images. And, incredibly, his illustrations for *Gargantua and Pantagruel* are as bawdy and fanciful as any imaginings set to paper by Rabelais.

Icart's literary tastes were certainly varied. In addition to the *livres d'artistes* he illustrated, his library contained works of Krafft-Ebing, De Sade, Freud, Poe, and other authors whose writings seem unlikely in the collection of an artist so often identified with the carefree and fanciful. But there was another side to Icart's nature, a fondness for mystery and a great interest in the inner psychological workings of man. While Icart's etchings and paintings seem coated with the patina of frivolity, many of his book illustrations reveal an insight that extended far beyond that expected of him by his critics.

The public responded eargerly to Icart's *livres d'artistes*. In some cases, his limited edition volumes sold for much more than his etchings. When *Le Sixième Mariage de*

Barbe-Bleue first appeared in 1938, the first five copies of an edition of two hundred sold for 4,000 francs each. The first twenty-five copies of *Dame aux Camélias* sold for 3,150 francs each. Subscribers were so eager for Icart's *livres d'artistes* that time-payment plans were established, permitting buyers to purchase a book over a period of one year at an interest rate of approximately 12 per cent. Despite the costs, sales were brisk, netting both artist and atelier a handsome profit.

Each illustrated book has its own special characteristics, both as a fine book and as a collection of original illustrations. Each work is examined individually here, and a chronological presentation traces the development of Icart as a master of the medium.

L'Ingénue Libertine by Gabrielle Colette, published in 1926, was Louis Icart's first major *livre d'artiste*. Originally the book was two works, titled *Minne*, by Colette's former husband, Willy, and *Les Égarements de Minne* by Colette. Upon mutual agreement, the two books were combined into one, bearing the name Colette Willy as authoress. This revision of the two books prompted Colette to encourage her friend, Louis Icart, to work with the master printers, Editions Excelsior, in the preparation of the book as a *livre d'artiste*. Icart, who had never illustrated a book prior to that time, agreed, selecting drypoint etching as a medium in which he would immortalize Minne's indiscretions. The young lady's faults of conduct were not that serious by today's standards (several random love affairs highlight the work), yet Icart found the story of this young girl's quest for sexual satisfaction and happiness a great opportunity to speculate on woman's search for love.

The twenty-five etchings in the book are clearly reminiscent of the etchings Icart produced for the American market. Many feature models who lounge on divans or before a fireplace or in other typically Icart poses (Fig. 153). The artist's Minne is both beautiful and sensual, and obviously inspired by Fanny. *L'Ingénue Libertine*, however, is not just a simple repeat of Icart's American market pieces—his etchings of Minne's discovery of her dead lover, for instance (Fig. 154), is a striking use of composition to display her grief and shame. The final plate in the book, in which pure lust powerfully grips Colette's heroine (Fig. 155), reveals that Icart who well understands the happy look on his model's face.

The etching line on most of these works is deep and the plates are rich with hand coloring. While drypoint line is the strongest element in use throughout the work, Icart also makes use of various other techniques; one notes, for example, the use of sugar lift to create the effect on the curtains in Figure 154.

In 1928, Icart expanded his role as a designer for the *livre d'artiste* when he created six etchings and ten woodcut initials for *Bigarrure*, a book of plays and stories by his friend Abel Hermant. Unlike many of the works Icart later produced for *livres d'artistes*, this small volume was not so much an artistic effort as a text supplemented with original graphics. The etchings are relatively small for a book of this type, measuring four by five inches, and again they are in keeping with the mood of the etchings produced for the American market. While the works are of interest for what they are—original etchings by Louis Icart (Figs. 156, 157)—the book itself bears little strength as an individual work of art.

In 1930, Editions Excelsior asked Icart to illustrate *Contemplations: La Fête Chez Thérèse* by Victor Hugo. Icart was reputed a Hugophile because of his membership in Paris organizations dedicated to the reading and study of works by Hugo. At once Icart's attentions were turned toward the lyrical eighteenth-century story of his literary idol. The resulting works—etchings with hand-colored palatial gardens, lute players, and elegant ladies—proved the artist's touch on copperplate was as delicate as the subject matter he had been commissioned to illustrate.

Figs. 154, 155. From *L'Ingénue Libertine*, drypoint and etching, 1926.

Figs. 156, 157. From *Bigarrure*, drypoint and etching, 1928.

155.

157.

Figs. 158-161. From *Le Sopha*, etching.

Icart himself was enthusiastic for additional experimentation with the *livre d'artiste*. Now that the American market had been sufficiently supplied with a backlog of etchings, the artist began to devote more time to an art form that became increasingly interesting to him.

Icart's next major book project was *Le Sopha* by Crebillon fils, an altogether

159.

160.

fanciful journey into an erotic tale of India. Originally published in 1740, the story concerns a young Indian prince and the various tales he is told by his courtesans. The twenty-three playful etchings created by Icart for this *livre d'artiste* reveal another phase of his erotic art, in which humor is as important as the implied or direct sexuality displayed. Invariably the beautiful courtesans cavort on rich, thick pillows (Fig. 158). The facial expressions in moments of dismay are typically Icart (Fig. 159), as are the suggestive situations and the sense of movement (Figs. 160, 161).

163.

Figs. 162-167. From *Gargantua and Pantagruel,* photogravure.

By far the artist's boldest illustrations to date, *Le Sopha* sold for 585 francs, a sum that put the book within financial reach of many collectors. Once the book was offered to subscribers of the publisher, Le Vasseur et Cie, the complete edition of 497 copies sold out quickly.

Icart turned to photomechanical reproduction processes in his next book, *Bug O'Shea,* by the French author Paul Morand, who examined Irish-American life in this work. The novel, with its emphasis on gangsters, suicide, and unhappiness, is probably Icart's poorest showing as a book illustrator. Obviously printed with a limited budget, the book reproduces Icart watercolors in a two-color process, and for several reasons, the pictures fail to evoke the strength shown in other Icart creations. Perhaps because the protagonist is a male, Icart was unable to deal successfully with the book. Also, the drawings are heavily caricatured, a feature which did not enhance *Bug O'Shea.*

It is no accident that Icart should have turned to *Gargantua and Pantagruel* as his next project. Like Rabelais's giant of medieval legend, which the author adapted as a satire on King Francis I in 1532, Icart himself enjoyed a robust and pleasure-filled life. The result was a five-volume book with seventy-six captivating, bawdy illustrations that follow the adventures of the giant Gargantua and his son, Pantagruel, as they lustfully make their way through the English countryside.

Icart's humor was in excellent form when he illustrated *Gargantua and Pantagruel.* Most of the illustrations are sexual jokes that are rich in *double entendre:* Figure 162 shows the aftermath of a hanging, and one may note with amusement the hemp plant that seems to be the source of the deadly rope; Figure 163 is a tribute to lusty drink, while Figure 164 is an irreverent image of three clerics who have left their ladies for the

128

164.

distant church. Figure 165 cleverly illustrates the old legend that the devil will be repulsed by those who expose their privates to him. Icart makes a joke of passing gas in the surrealistic Figure 166; one must look closely at the two naked lovers in Figure 167 to notice the nearby habit and priestly robe.

The blatant sexuality and jokes based on bodily functions made this book shocking for even the publisher's subscribers. But wisely, Le Vasseur anticipated a great demand for the volumes and printed a large edition of nearly 1,000 copies.

Icart took special care in preparing this work. An early number of the edition, specially prepared as a gift for a friend, featured hand-tooled leather bindings designed and executed by Icart. Each cover features the face of the giant Gargantua as he progressively devours a cow. Icart played cartoonist to the limit of his work, and the result was brilliant.

165.

166.

167.

Figs, 168, 169. From *La Dame aux Camelias,* etching.

The great nineteenth-century romance, *Dame aux Camélias* by Alexander Dumas *fils*, gave Louis Icart another great opportunity to employ his talents as a graphic artist of the book. Prepared several years after Mme. Claudia Victrix's performance as Marguerite Gautier in the 1933 stage production, this *livre d'artiste* features twenty-five etchings modeled after the actress and her interpretation of the famous Dumas heroine.

While the style of these etchings is again similar in many respects to Icart's exported works, they are in many ways more apropos as book illustrations. By illustrating this tale of the early nineteenth century, Icart found himself in the romantic element best suited to his talents. *Dame aux Camélias* is Icart's poem to the elegant grace of both Mme Victrix and Marguerite Gautier.

Written in 1848 when Dumas was twenty-three, *Dame aux Camélias* was one of the author's earliest successes. It is the basis for his 1882 drama and for Giuseppe Verdi's opera, *La Traviata*. It concerns Armand Duval who begins a doomed love affair with the courtesan Marguerite.

Again, Icart's illustrations for this work do not vary greatly from the full-sized etchings he produced for export. While some plates display an unexpected eroticism, Marguerite's deathbed scene for instance, most are pastel sentiments in which colors are kept to a minimum and the liberal use of white is distinctive (Figs. 168, 169). In twenty-five sensitive, beautiful etchings, Icart made perhaps his most sentimental and most touching tribute to "romantic love."

Still another side of Louis Icart revealed itself in *Le Sixième Mariage de Barbe-Bleue* written by Charles Perrault in 1697. Icart's somber, mysterious illustrations for this tale of terror are rich in subtle shadows and ominous images. The tale concerns the Chevalier Raoul, who has forbidden his new bride to enter certain rooms in his castle. Of course she cannot resist the temptation to explore, and when she enters the forbidden area, she finds the bodies of the Chevalier's other wives. Luckily, she escapes the fate of her predecessors, but not before several harrowing incidents.

Choosing to avoid the direct horrors of the murders in his illustrations, Icart concentrated on female beauty, utilizing expressive composition and shading to achieve the mood of mystery that dominates the work. The movement in some of the etchings depends heavily on background (Fig. 170), the flow of a gown (Fig. 171), or other dramatic accessories for a total visual effect (Fig. 172).

Le Sixième Mariage de Barbe-Bleue is also significant because it marks the beginning of a close relationship between Icart and Charles Meunier, one of the finest master printers in France. Icart and Meunier would collaborate on several other books and almost without exception they represent the artist's finest *livre d'artiste* creations.

Icart's next *livre d'artiste* is of particular interest because only one copy exists. *La Femme de Marbre* by Henri de Régnier, features thirty monotypes created by the artist as a gift for his wife. The book was typeset, cut, and boxed, with Fanny as the sole recipient. It is a puzzling gift. The idealized beauty extends itself here to the sculptor Demetrios, who loves the beautiful Chrysis, a courtesan of Tyre. His desire for Chrysis is overpowering. As a price for her favors, Chrysis demands that Demetrios bring gifts that he must steal from Pharaoh at great risk. He scorns her after he succeeds in obtaining the items, and creates a statue which represents her. Chrysis finally poisons herself after she realizes the mockery she has made of their love, and Demetrios then smashes the statue.

Icart's illustrations trace the figure of Chrysis from childhood, when she first enters the city (Fig. 173), to her attempted seduction of Pharaoh (Fig. 175), and finally to her bizarre attraction to the statue of herself (Fig. 174). One can only conjecture as

Figs. 170-172. From *Le Sixième Mariage de Barbe-Bleue*, drypoint.

171.

172.

Figs. 173-175. From *La Femme de Marbre,* etching.

174.

175.

Fig. 176. From *Chrysis*, drypoint and etching, 1940.

to the meaning this strange story held for Louis and Fanny. Perhaps this is a mystery lost in the flames that devoured Fanny Icart's secrets.

Icart later illustrated *Chrysis* as a *livre d'artiste,* this time based on the novel *Aphrodite* by Pierre Louÿs. These illustrations, executed in 1940, are among the artist's most effective interpretations of female beauty. The soft coloring and clean lines define the human form with a limited number of strokes, giving the work a modern look while still maintaining the classic character of the story. Chrysis entering her bath, or Chrysis in a pose of exquisite ecstasy (Fig. 176), is among the artist's most graceful females.

One may wonder how the occupation of Paris by the German forces may have affected the creation of *livres d'artistes.* In truth, the Occupation was an encouragement to the creation of such books. The Germans, whose censors were especially strict, banned the production of erotic books of any type. The French, who had come to regard the *livre d'artiste* as an expressly French art form, continued secret production of such books despite the restrictions. Art supplies such as painting materials were in scarce supply, and few galleries were exhibiting works. Book publishing came to a near standstill, and the *livre d'artiste*—a small edition selling for a high price—provided a way for publishers to earn capital. The *livre d'artiste* offered a practical means of investment for speculators, and there were still enough wealthy French who could afford to speculate on fine books.

Icart's World War II book production decreased, mainly because of the erotic and political nature of the works he illustrated. One of his first Occupation book efforts was the book of monotypes from *L'Exode.* Executed at the same time he did the

Figs. 177, 178. From *Léda*, drypoint and etching, 1943.

178.

paintings on this theme, *L'Exode* is a simple volume of fifty plates that duplicate the oil paintings. The monotypes are printed in black with traces of red, and while they have inherent strength as works of art, they do not match the power of the paintings on the same theme.

After the initial turmoil of the Occupation, Icart again returned to the illustration of erotic books. In 1943, he completed illustrations for *Léda* by Pierre Louÿs. The theme of Leda and the swan was irresistible for Icart. A theme he had interpreted in both etching and painting, this book version of the bizarre love story allowed him to express the tale with simple, quickly executed etchings. Whether his Leda is faced with the satyr or the swan, she easily succumbs to her sensual predispositions.

The small volume is typical of many French *livres d'artistes* created during the Occupation in that it is not especially sumptuous, and the small edition of 147 examples made it available only to a highly select group of buyers.

Much of the simplicity Icart had developed in *Chrysis* remained in *Léda,* although the artist returned again to shadings and detail in the etching line. Leda's ecstasy (Fig. 177) is graphically portrayed. Icart also used the work to reintroduce the satyr seen in some early etchings (Fig. 178), a figure that Icart often used to caricature himself. The artist may well have fancied himself the sexual daredevil epitomized by the cloven-hoofed satyr. Many of the satyrs he used in illustrations and etchings bear a resemblance to himself, and in a series of fifty pornographic etchings—done by Icart in the early 1920s—which feature a satyr with two receptive ladies, the similarity is particularly striking.

Later that same year, Icart provided illustrations for Johann von Goethe's *Faust.* A number of Icart's *Faust* illustrations display a semiabstract quality, and the works created for the book are less realistic and highly successful interpretations of the Goethe tale.

Icart's illustrations for *Faust* are printed by photogravure a technique that permitted him to closely duplicate the immediate feeling of his monotypes. *Faust* is more colorful than most of Icart's *livres d'artistes*, but it is also more dreamlike and, at times, decidedly bizarre. Four skeletal women stand before an ominous staircase (Fig. 179). Several dark, mysterious figures lower a body into a grave (Fig. 180) and the

Figs. 179–181. *Faust*, photogravure, 1944.

180.

181.

image becomes one of a giant feasting spider. A dream on a hilltop (Fig. 181) is alive with swirling images of nudes.

After the liberation of Paris in August 1944, Icart illustrated *Destin de Femme* by Thérèse Castel, a novel about the Occupation and the effect on the life of a young woman. The contemporary novel, published as a *livre d'artiste,* ends tragically with the heroine's suicide, an unhappy commentary on the fate of woman during wartime.

At times, Icart's hand-colored etchings seem incompatible with the mood of this novel. In illustrating this contemporary tragedy, the artist was unable to escape his penchant for humor. And in technique, he attempted to blend many of the oil painting techniques of *les visions blanches* with the aquatint illustrations here. His etching work is not as detailed as in previous books. The figures are sketchy and the backgrounds are soft and pastel. The lines are spare and suggestive, highlighting only the most important definitive features. A woman putting on lipstick (Fig. 182), a figure in a doorway (Fig. 183), and lovers on a hilltop (Fig. 184) are loosely drawn, a departure from his usual technique. In this work, Icart succeeds best in the small chapter headings which readily establish a mood without the necessity for precise storytelling.

Icart next turned to a subject with which he was very familiar. *La Vie des Seins,* by Docteur Jacobus, features fifteen full-page etchings and fifteen *culs-de-lampes* showing the female breast in all its forms and fashions.

Again the artist employed drypoint with only an essential touch of color in each illustration. The erotic content of the illustrations is strong (Figs. 185-187), showing that this master of eroticism did not lack feeling for such specialized subject matter. The text of *La Vie des Seins* is a pseudoscientific study of various breast formations, attributed to one Docteur Jacobus, who was actually Icart himself writing under a pseudonym.

Figs. 182-184. From *Destin de Femme,* etching, 1945.   183.

184.

Fig. 185. From *La Vie des Seins*, drypoint, 1945.

Louis Icart turned to a tale of the eighteenth century, *La Nuit et le Moment* by Crebillon, for his next *livre d'artiste*. Known as *Opportunities of a Night*, this tale concerns the adventures of various couples whose couplings at an elegant estate produce several amusing situations. Icart's illustrations for this work are of particular interest because they duplicate the style of Fragonard's illustrations for *Les Contes de la Fontaine*, published in 1780. The etching lines are spare in the Icart work, as they are in Fragonard's, and the hand coloring is added lightly, with a mind to immediacy. Most scenes depict frenzied seductions (Figs. 188, 189), or just plain provocative languor (Fig. 190). The stylistic achievements make this one of Icart's most sensuous *livres d'artistes*.

Icart's foremost accomplishment as an illustrator of the *livre d'artiste* was realized in 1947 with the publication of *Les Fleurs du Mal* by Charles Baudelaire. Limited to a small edition of only twenty-one copies, the work successfully translates the haunting poetry of Baudelaire's most famous work into visual terms. Every aspect of the book is a tribute to the art of fine bookmaking. With a special typeface designed by Charles Meunier, slipcase and covers made of finest oriental papers, and careful attention to layout, *Les Fleurs du Mal* was several months in preparation.

When the poems were originally published in June 1857, Baudelaire was tried and convicted of blasphemy and obscenity, and six of the poems—those dealing with incest and other unpopular themes—were banned in France until 1949. Icart, from respect for Baudelaire and partly in defiance of the ridiculous censorship, insisted that the poems be included in the work, making it even more daring, in many respects, than previous *livres d'artistes* by the artist.

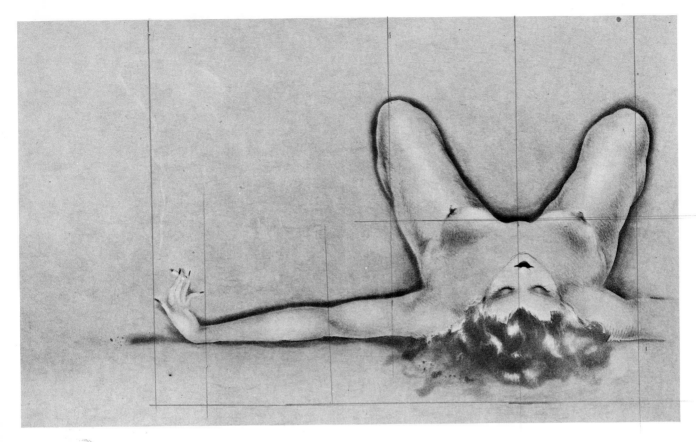

Figs. 186-187. From *La Vie des Seins*, drypoint, 1945.

187.

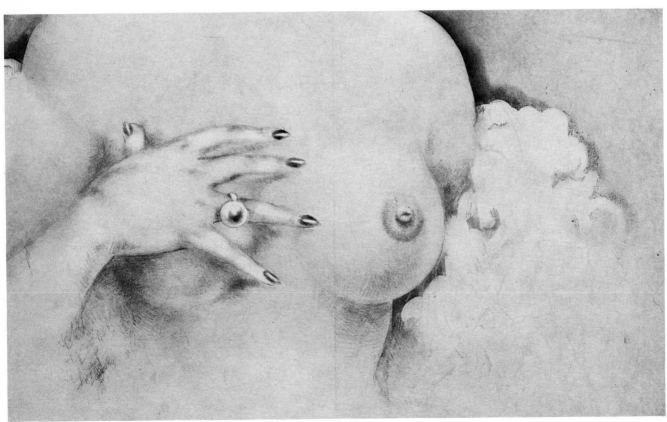

Figs. 188-190. From *La Nuit et le Moment* (Opportunities of a Night), drypoint, 1946.

189.

190.

Fig. 192. *Spleen,* from *Les Fleurs du Mal,* watercolor, 1947.

Fig. 191. Title illustration for *Les Fleurs du Mal,* lithograph, 1947.

Fig. 193. *Spleen,* from *Les Fleurs du Mal,* lithograph, 1947.

Fig. 196. *La Géante,* from *Les Fleurs du Mal,* lithograph, 1947.

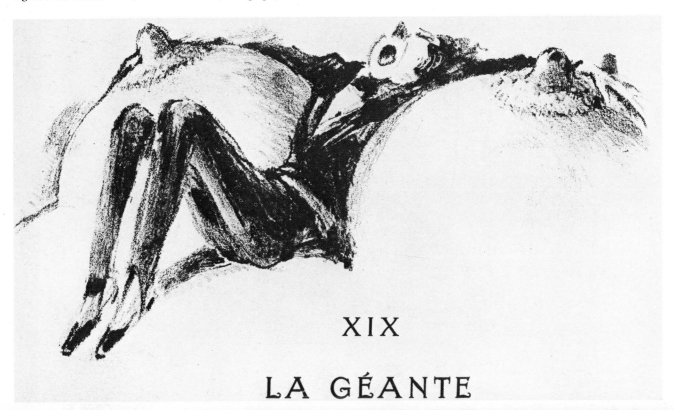

XIX

LA GÉANTE

Fig. 194. *Bénédiction*, from *Les Fleurs du Mal*, watercolor, 1947.

Fig. 195. *Bénédiction*, from *Les Fleurs du Mal*, lithograph, 1947.

The lithographic illustrations are haunting. They owe this quality in part to the use of the lithographic stone. Icart's interpretations of death, greed, and shame are as powerful as any illustrations ever prepared for the Baudelaire masterpiece. Even the title page of the work, which bears the artist's pencil signature, features traditional Icart images of female beauty, set into a diabolic bouquet of vipers, spiders, and other assorted images of terror (Fig. 191).

The edition of twenty-one volumes also contains an *exemplaire unique* in which the artist first illustrated the planned ideas with wash; the placement of the illustrations being established, he proceeded to the stone for the twenty other books in the edition. After creating the wash drawing, Icart made few changes in the resulting lithographs. The wash illustration for the poem *Spleen* (Fig. 192) is followed directly by the lithograph (Fig. 193), although the mood of the work is certainly more sinister and mysterious on stone. *Bénédiction*, in which Icart drew an older woman in the wash illustration (Fig. 194) was altered as a lithograph (Fig. 195) to portray the woman as a young girl. *Les Fleurs du Mal* is not without humor, as is seen in *La Géante* (Fig. 196), nor the unmistakable presence of Fanny, as seen in *La Beauté* (Fig. 197).

Fig. 197. *La Beauté*, from *Les Fleurs du Mal*, lithograph, 1947.

XVII

LA BEAUTÉ

Truly the most sumptuous and significant *livre d'artiste* created by Louis Icart, *Les Fleurs du Mal* is the ideal synthesis of written and illustrated poetry.

Icart's next *livre d'artiste* gave him another opportunity to display his feeling for the eighteenth century. *Félicia ou Mes Fredaines* by Andrea de Nerciat is a bawdy novel in which courtly gentlemen seduce and dally with the ladies of the Court. It is a robust story, complete with wanton women (Figs. 198, 199) and unconventional sexual encounters (Figs. 200, 201).

Icart did not try to do Fragonardlike illustrations for this work. Instead he reverted to the form of etching employed in *Destin de Femme*. The colors are soft, and the etching line is quick, a quality that works well in the baroque images created by the artist. Humor is a strong element of *Félicia*, as seen in the eager coupling of the butler and the maid (Fig. 201), and Icart's wit and imagination help to capture the flavor of the eighteenth century at its most sexually adventurous.

Icart's next *livre d'artiste* was *Les Chansons de Bilitis*, published in 1949 as one volume in a series of five major works by Pierre Louÿs. The other four volumes were illustrated by various *peintres-graveurs*, with each book being printed in an edition of 1,720 copies. First published in Paris in 1894, *Les Chansons de Bilitis* is based on the poetry of Sappho, the Greek poetess of Lesbos, whose works date to 600 B.C.

Icart found his talents easily adaptable to the highly erotic nature of this work. Throughout the book Icart adopted a loose, sketchy style which is at times similar to the work of Marcel Vertès, who became a pacesetter of feminine beauty in the 1940s, much as Icart had been in the 1920s. The works were executed in pen and photomechanically produced on the page in black. Under careful guidance of the artist, each illustration was then hand-colored by Albert Jon, who was on the staff of the editor, Albin Michel. A watercolor sketch that Icart executed for the title page of *Les Chansons de Bilitis* (Fig. 202) leaves little to the imagination concerning the nature of the work. In some earlier book illustrations, and even in some etchings exported to the United States, the innuendos about Lesbian love existed—the playful duet near a screen, the girlish whisper, the joyful teasing at a fishbowl. But while Icart could never fully explore the subject in these works, he could approach the subject with disarming candor in a *livre d'artiste*, which was directed at a population of buyers who were much more willing to accept the reality of lesbianism.

Les Amours de Psyche et de Cupidon by Jean de la Fontaine was Icart's final *livre d'artiste*, a work limited to only one hundred and fifty copies. The twenty-four etchings which make up the illustrations are erotic and subtly beautiful. After all his years as an illustrator of *livres d'artistes*, the master had not lost his touch in this final work.

Looking back at the nature of the *livres d'artistes* created by Louis Icart reveals an artist with a hunger for artistic expression of all types. Unfinished at the time of Icart's death were the illustrations for a book that was more bizarre than any he had thus far completed—*L'Hermaphrodite* by Edmond Cazel—which was an unrealized dream that may have revealed yet another phase of Icart's prodigious talent.

Figs. 198-201. From *Félicia ou Mes Fredaines*, etching, 1947.

199.

200.

201.

Fig. 202. From *Les Chansons de Bilitis*, sketch, pencil, and watercolor, 1949.

Figures 203–204 appear on page 148

Club des Cent

Tout ça ?... Jamais !

05.

CHAPTER 6

THE RENAISSANCE MAN

EVERY ASPECT OF LOUIS ICART'S LIFE WAS TOUCHED BY HIS ART. WHEN ICART TURNED TO THE theatre as a creative byway, he not only became reader and poet, but costume and set designer. To calm his nerves and to take his mind away from business pressures, he sketched Fanny and her roses. Even the act of preparing a meal became for Icart another opportunity to put his artistic abilities to work.

As a member of the *Club des Cent*, the exclusive gourmet society, he was not content merely to enjoy the fine food and wine. Icart joined with other members to produce imaginative delicacies, and, more important, to design clever menu covers for the special dinners. Limited to editions of less than 125, the menus were hand-signed etchings by the artist, and they were given as souvenirs to each member attending the feast.

The artist was particularly suggestive here in his subject matter, frequently relating the female figure on the cover to some specialty of the evening. A fish dinner, for example, resulted in a menu cover called *La Pêche* (Fishing), (Fig. 203), showing an unsuspecting fisherman with a spectacular catch. Another menu featured a distraught lady whose petticoats have been invaded by numerous uninvited visitors (Fig. 204).

Club des Cent menus always maintained the Icart humor, even in the most difficult

Figs. 203-207. Menu covers for *Club des Cent,* drypoint, 6 x 7½. 204.

times. A 1940 menu, created just before the invasion of France, shows a French demoiselle in armor with sword, ready to defend her land from the attackers. Each city on the map behind her features the name of a food product native to the area, and the caption reads, "Everything? Never!" (Fig. 205). A more solemn, though hopeful menu, executed during the Occupation, pictures a girl with a dove before the ominous shadow of a soldier and cannon (Fig. 206). After the liberation of Paris in 1944, Icart created a glorious menu which shows a tank whose gun has been silenced with a champagne cork, while the flags of the Allies wave nearby (Fig. 207).

Another leisure-time activity—Icart's sketching of Fanny—sparked the creation of *Dessins de Femmes* a 1928 portfolio of twenty-four lithographs based on these sketches. Drawn directly on lithographic stones and printed in black, the artist later highlighted each work in the edition of 500 with pastel crayon. The works are so much like his original sketches that they resemble original drawings, a matter of some confusion to today's collectors who could easily mistake any of the lithographs for a one-of-a-kind piece. These lithographs were all signed within the stone; the portfolio was distributed intact within France, but not intended for general distribution in the United States, although some numbers did find their way to this country.

Each illustration depicts the female figure in a typical Icart pose: a girl in a masquerade costume (Fig. 208), a lady with a puppet (Fig. 209), a seminude in a lace shawl (Fig. 210), a girl with a cockatoo (Fig. 211). While the sketchy quality in no way matches the detail to be found in Icart's etchings, the master's touch is clearly evident.

Many of these same scenes were later reproduced as large original crayon drawings measuring up to five feet in height. Icart had been commissioned to create window pieces for the Wanamaker department store in New York City and the artist's freehand work found a suitable outlet in such a large format. The large drawings were never used in Wanamaker displays, but similar pieces created for shops in Paris did make their way into display windows (Figs. 212-214).

In the late 1940s Icart renewed his love for the theatre. A decade earlier, he had found a means of expression in *Don Quichotte de la Manche.* Not only had the artist written the script, he had provided the sets and costume designs. His next play, *Rabelais,* was never actually produced, but Icart had prepared extensive notes on settings and costumes. The costume sketches he executed for *Rabelais* were prepared in watercolor. They feature a wide range of personalities—from a colorful priest (Fig. 215) to a miserable beggar (Fig. 216). Though meant strictly as costume designs, the artist could not resist the addition of facial characteristics and personalities to his sketches.

The final work selected for inclusion in this volume is Icart's lithographic poster for *Dame aux Camélias,* created in 1933. This sensitive, beautiful work featured Claudia Victrix in a standing position, while a lover knelt at her feet. A special edition of the poster, before the addition of lettering, was prepared by Icart for distribution among friends and for sale in the galleries that handled his work. The unlettered lithograph was limited to an edition of fifty impressions. Icart rarely produced posters, but this particular work shows his ability to handle that medium as gracefully as he handled the etchings (Fig. 217). In many ways, the figures in the poster anticipate Icart's illustrations for his *livre d'artiste* of the same work by Dumas *fils.* In the book, as in the poster, Mme Victrix was the obvious inspiration.

In time, as Icart's oil paintings, watercolors, and illustrated books find their way into the art marketplace and into galleries and museums, the artist's total output will be evaluated and—hopefully—appreciated. Icart's works represent more than a momentary pleasure; he fashioned the dreams of an era into a tangible reality, and for this he will be remembered.

206.

207.

-211. Lithographs from *Dessins des Femmes*,
x 18.

209.

210.

211.

Figs. 212-214. Display drawings for Wanamaker's department store, circa 1925, approximately 24 x 60.

213.

214.

Figs. 215, 216. Costume sketches for *Rabelais*, watercolor, circa 1945, 8 x 10.

Fig. 217. Poster for *La Dame aux Camelias*, lithograph, 1933, 46 x 62.

ETCHINGS, OIL PAINTINGS,
AND OTHER WORKS BY LOUIS ICART
REGISTERED WITH THE
UNITED STATES OFFICE OF COPYRIGHT

The following list is designed to aid collectors in identifying and naming works by Louis Icart. Only a portion of the artist's great output was registered with the United States Office of Copyright: those works created for distribution in America and those oil paintings that were reproduced as prints are included in this listing.

Copyrights were generated by a variety of sources. The earliest copyrights were obtained by galleries that distributed Icart's works in the United States, for example, the F. H. Bresler Company in Milwaukee, Wisconsin. *L'Estampe Moderne,* and *Les Gravures Modernes,* two Parisian publishers of Icart's works, were the prime sources of copyrights during the mid to late 1920s. After the formation of the Louis Icart Society, that organization generated all the copyrights. In many instances, however, Louis Icart himself registered copyrights.

Copyright sources are generally listed on the top right or left border of the etching image. While copyright protections have expired on certain works, a number of American copyrights were renewed by Fanny Icart after her husband's death and those protections are still active. Additionally, all the artist's works are protected by French copyright laws for fifty years after the artist's death; international copyright agreements make certain French laws applicable in this country.

A note must be made regarding the nomenclature of Louis Icart's etchings. The artist named most of the works in French, but American designations were often given by the distributor or individual galleries, a procedure that resulted in several titles for the same work. Many gallery owners inscribed the American or French name of the work in the lower right margin. When possible, the following list gives all the names attributed to Icart's works. French names are listed first, alphabetically, followed by their American counterparts. Not all names from the French were translated literally, and in some instances, where an American name seemed most appropriate for a work, no French title was given.

In preparing this list I have endeavored to list both etching sizes and editions. Sizes indicated are of the image area, and are approximate to the half-inch. Editions have been indicated only when published sources, such as gallery catalogs, have listed them.

One final note: Copyright dates indicated in this listing are the registration dates at the U. S. Copyright Office in Washington, D.C., and they may not always conform to the copyright dates printed on the etchings themselves. I advise, therefore, checking both the year previous and year after the copyright date printed on the etching, when attempting to determine the title of a particular piece. Additionally, although many works bear copyright dates, no record of these works exists in Washington, and they have therefore not been included in this listing.

Measurements are of the image area to the nearest half-inch, horizontal dimension first.
(-o)—oval
(-c)—cathedral

EDITION	DATE	FRENCH OR ORIGINAL TITLE	AMERICAN TITLE OR TITLES	SIZE
	1911	*Au Jardin de Paris*	Parisian Gardens	
		Edmée		
	1914	*Le Bain*	The Bath	
		Bouquet	Bouquet	
75		*Coursing*	Coursing I	16 x 11½
		Le Divan	The Divan	14½ x 11½
		Flirtation	Flirtation	
75		*Le Golf*	Golf	11 x 17
		Le Manchon	The Muff	
75		*Le Papillon*	The Butterfly	11 x 19
75		*Premiers Beaux Jours*	First Beautiful Days	9½ x 15
75		*Vision Printanière*	Springtime Vision	11½ x 18½
100	**1918**	*L'As Vainquer*	Winged Victory	15 x 21½
75		*Marianne*	La Marseillaise	12 x 19½
300	**1921**	*Le Cacatoès Indiscret*	The Indiscreet Cockatoo	11 x 13-o
300	**1922**	*Le Bandeau*	The Blindfold	17½ x 14½
300		*Cage Vide*	The Open Cage	12½ x 18
		Colombes	The Doves	13½ x 14½
300		*Cruche Cassée*	The Broken Jug	12½ x 18½-o
300		*Derrière L'Eventail*	*Behind the Fan*	*19 x 14⁴-o*
		Fatigué	Weary	19 x 13½-o
		Marionnettes	Puppets	18½ x 15-o
		Les Masques	Japanese Masks	
300		*La Paravent de Laque*	The Lacquer Screen	
	1923	*En Auto, Automobilisme*	Motorcar	18½ x 14
		Minauche	Minauche	11 x 14-o
		Le Bouddha Bleu	Blue Buddha	19 x 13½-o
	1924	*La Cruche Cassée*	Broken Jug	11½ x 17-o
		La Falque	Wistfulness	17 x 11
		Petite Prisonnière	Little Prisoner	19 x 15
		Poissons Japonais	Japanese Goldfish	17½ x 13½-o
		La Poupée	Baby Doll	17½ x 13-o
	1925	*L'Averse*	Rain, The Shower	14 x 18½-o
		Avant le Raid	Before the Attack	21 x 17½
		Le Châle Noir	The Black Shawl	12½ x 16½
		Coup de Vent	Gust of Wind	17½ x 21
		Décembre	December	14½ x 19½
		Les Eléphants	Elephants	11½ x 16½
		Les Oiseaux Bleues	Bluebirds	15½ x 19
		Le Paon	The Peacock	15 x 18½
350		*Paresse*	Laziness	19 x 15
		Petits Chats	Kittens	21½ x 16½-o
		Petits Chiens	Puppies	21½ x 16½-o
350		*Sur le Divan*	White Underwear	19 x 15
350		*Sur l'Herbe*	In the Open	16 x 10½
350		*Sur le Sable*	On the Beach	16 x 10½
	1926	*Les Ailes Blanches*	White Wings	11½ x 16½
		L'Aumone	Alms	12½ x 17-o
		Bavardage	Gossip	13 x 16½-o
350		*La Bonne Histoire*	The Storyteller	17 x 14-o
		Le Bouddha en Colère	The Angry Buddha	17½ x 21½-o
350		*La Cage Ouverte*	The Open Cage	13 x 17-o
		Les Chatons	Kittens	9½ x 10
		La Confidence	The Confidence	20½ x 16-o

EDITION	DATE	FRENCH OR ORIGINAL TITLE	AMERICAN TITLE OR TITLES	SIZE
350		*Effronterie*	Effrontery, Impudence	13½ x 18-o
		L'Etreinte	The Embrace	17 x 14-o
		Femme aux Raisins	Woman with Grapes	19½ x 14
350		*Feuilles d'Automne*	Autumn Leaves	16 x 20-o
		Fruit Défendu	Forbidden Fruit	13 x 17½
		Les Fruits	Fruit	
		Fumée	Smoke	20 x 15
	1926	*Gavotte*	Gavotte	
		Il m'aime	He loves me	12 x 16½
		Le Gué	Crossing	13½ x 19
		Les Hirondelles	Swallows	13 x 17
		Les Juillards	Birds of July	13 x 17
		Leçon de Chant	Singing Lesson	18 x 14-o
350		*Lettres d'Amour*	Love Letters	17½ x 14-o
350		*Les Masques*	The Masks	15 x 18½-o
350		*Les Mouettes*	Seagulls	16 x 20-o
350		*Nuit Espagnole*	Spanish Night	13 x 21-c
350		*Nuit Vénitienne*	Venetian Night	13 x 21-c
		Petits Papillons	Little Butterflies, Butter-fly Falls	
		Petite Jalousie	The Small Screen	
		Les Pillards	The Thieves	
		Ponvoites	Desire	
350		*Poupée Moderne*	French Doll	18 x 14-o
350		*La Robe de Chine*	The Silk Robe, The Silk Dress	18½ x 15
		Taquinerie	Teasing	13½ x 18-o
		Tendre Leçon	The Tender Lesson	
		Le Thé	The Tea	14½ x 18½-o
		Les Trésors	Treasures	11 x 9-o
	1927	*Attente*	Waiting	14 x 13½-o
		Au Clair de la Lune	By Moonlight, Pierrette	13½ x 20½
		Au Revoir	Farewell	19 x 14½
500		*La Belle au Bois Dormant*	Sleeping Beauty	19½ x 15½-o
		Butterfly	Madame Butterfly	13 x 20
		La Cachette	The Hiding Place	14½ x 18
		Carmen	Carmen	13½ x 20
500		*Le Chaperon Rouge*	Red Riding Hood	14 x 21
500		*Cendrillon*	Cinderella	18 x 14½-o
		La Dame aux Camélias	Lady of the Camelias	21 x 17-o
		Les Espiègles	Mischievous	20 x 16-o
		Fidélité	Fidelity	
		Il Pleut Bergère	Bo Peep, Shepherdess in the Rain	14 x 21-o
		Jalousie	Jealousy	
		Leçon d'Amour	Lesson of Love	10 x 9½
	1927	*Louise*	Louise	13 x 20
500		*Manon*	Manon	13 x 20
		Mimi	Mimi	13 x 20
		Mimi Pinson	Mimi Pinson	20½ x 13½
		Miss America	Miss America	13 x 20-o
		Miss California	Miss California	13 x 20-o
		Musette	Musetta	13 x 20
		Le Petit Déjeuner	Mealtime	13½ x 17½-o

EDITION	DATE	FRENCH OR ORIGINAL TITLE	AMERICAN TITLE OR TITLES	SIZE
		La Réussite	Success	18½ x 14½-o
500		*Scheherezade*	Scheherazade	20 x 13
		Tentation	Temptation	14 x 19
500		*Thaïs*	Thaïs	20 x 16-o
500	1928	*Automne*	Autumn	6½ x 9
500		*Cage Rouge*	The Red Cage	9 x 11-o
500		*Casanova*	Casanova	14 x 21
		Coursing, Vitesse	Coursing, Speed	25 x 15½
		Dans les Branches, L'Escarpolette	The Swing	13½ x 19
		Dans les Passés	Recollections	17 x 12
		Dans les Rêves	Meditation	17 x 12
500		*Don Juan*	Don Juan	14 x 21
		Ecoute	Listen, Secrets	14 x 18-o
500		*L'Elan*	Zest	14 x 19
500		*L'Eté*	Summer	6½ x 9
		Eve	Eve	19½ x 14-o
500		*Faust*	Faust	13 x 21-c
		Feuilles d'Automne	Autumn Leaves	
500		*L'Hiver*	Winter	6½ x 9
500		*Intimité*	Intimacy, The Green Screen	18 x 16
500		*Marchande de Fleurs*	Flower Vendor	14 x 19
500		*Marchande de Marrons*	Chestnut Vendor	14 x 19
500		*Mignon*	Mignon	13½ x 20
500		*Montmartre*	Montmartre I	14½ x 21
100		*Moquerie*	Mockery, Red Screen	18 x 16
500		*Le Nid Renversé*	Fallen Nest	15 x 18½
500		*Le Panier Renversé*	Spilled Apples	12½ x 19½
500		*Perroquet Vert*	The Green Parakeet	9 x 11
500	1928	*Perroquet Bleu*	The Blue Parakeet	9 x 11
		Le Poème	The Poem	22 x 18
500		*Le Pot au Lait, La Laitière*	Milkmaid	12½ x 19½
500		*Premières Cérises*	The Parasol, First Cherries	14 x 17½-o
500		*Printemps*	Spring	6½ x 9
		Regarde	Look	14 x 18-o
		Salomé	Salome	13 x 20
500		*Séville*	Seville	13 x 20
		Tennis	Tennis	14 x 19
500		*Tosca*	Tosca	13 x 21-c
		Venus	Venus	19½ x 14-o
500		*Werther*	Werther	13 x 20
	1929	*Abat-jour, Pique-Nique*	Picnic	
		L'Alcôve Bleue	The Blue Alcove, Blue Divan	13 x 10½-o
		L'Alcôve Rose, Le Divan Rose	The Pink Alcove, Pink Divan	13 x 10½-o
		Ballet	Ballet	13 x 20
		La Biche Apprivoisée	Four Dears, Tamed Hind	15 x 21
		Chien et Chat	Cat and Dog, Dear Friends	11 x 14-o
		Colère	The Angry One	
		La Colombe Blessée	The Wounded Dove	16 x 21
		Conchita	Conchita	14 x 21

EDITION	DATE	FRENCH OR ORIGINAL TITLE	AMERICAN TITLE OR TITLES	SIZE
350		*Coursing II*	Coursing II	25 x 15½
		Dalila	Dalilah	13½ x 20½
		Danse Apache	Apache Dancer	13 x 20½
		Danse Espagnole	Spanish Dancer	13 x 20½
		1830	1830	18 x 14½-o
		1930	1930	18 x 14½-o
		Duo	Duet	13½ x 18-o
		Les Hortensias	Hydrangeas, Lilacs	21 x 17-o
		Jeanne d'Arc	Joan of Arc	14½ x 19
		La Jeune Mère	Young Mother, Mother and Child	15½ x 11½
		Joie de Vivre	Joy of Life	15 x 23½
		Madame Bovary	Madame Bovary	20 x 16-o
		Marchande d'Oranges	Orange Seller	14 x 19-o
	1929	*Marchande d'Oiseaux*	Bird Seller	14 x 19-o
		Menuet	Minuet	13 x 21
		Mon Chien	Dollar, My Dog	8 x 8
		Notre-Dame	Notre Dame	6 x 12½
		Place Vendôme	Place Vendome	6 x 12½
		Retour de Promenade	After the Walk	
		Salomé	Salome	13 x 20
		Sapho	Sappho	20 x 16
		Sur les Quais	Along the Quais	6 x 12½
	1930	*Arc en Ciel*	Rainbow	17 x 25
		Boudeuse	The Settee, Sulking	17 x 12
		Les Bulles	Bubbles	13½ x 18-o
		Convoitise	Covetousness	
		Coursing III	Coursing III	26 x 16
		Les Duos	Duets	
		Fleurs de Paris	Paris Flowers	19 x 15
		Les Frileux	The Chilly Ones	
		Le Gouter	The Snack	13½ x 17½-o
		Des Grieux	The Lovers	14 x 21
		Jeunesse	Youth	15½ x 24
		Méditation	Golden Veil	20 x 15
		Parasol	Parasol	
		Robe Rose	Pink Dress	
		Les Trileux	Birdsong, The Robin	14 x 19-o
	1931	*Baigneuses*	Bathing Beauties	17 x 24½
		Cigarette	Memories	18 x 15-o
		Danseuse	Dancer	18½ x 15
		D'Artagnan	D'Artagnan	14 x 21
		Eventail Noir	Black Fan	21 x 16-o
		L'Oiseau Blanc	White Bird	15 x 27
		L'Oiseau dans la Tempête	Bird in the Tempest	15 x 27
		Le Souvenir	The Souvenir	19½ x 16½
		La Vague	Venus in the Waves	16 x 19
		Les Yeux	Two Beauties	24 x 17
	1932	*Accord Parfait*	Perfect Harmony	16½ x 12½
		Au Repose (oil)	Dancer	
		Au Téléphone	Hello	
		Blancheurs	Symphony in White	15½ x 20
		Carnaval (oil)	Carnaval	
		Le Chat Qui Dort (oil)	Sleeping Cat	
		Cocktail	Cocktail, Martini	16½ x 12½

EDITION	DATE	FRENCH OR ORIGINAL TITLE	AMERICAN TITLE OR TITLES	SIZE
		Le Coquillage (oil)	Song of the Sea	
		Les Cygnes (oil)	The Swans	
		Dans les Rêves (oil)	Meditation	
		Eve (oil)	Eve	
		Fleurs de Nice	Spring Blossoms	15 x 23
		Fleurs des Champs (oil)	Flower Seller	
		Joie de Vivre (oil)	Joy of Life	
		Lilas et Roses (oil)	Lilacs and Roses	
		Madame Claudia Victrix (oil)	Madame Claudia Victrix	
		Les Masques	Masks	
		Matin d'Avril	April Morning	
		Modèle	My Model	16½ x 21
		Paravent de Laque (oil)	Lacquer Screen	
		Poissons Chinois	Chinese Goldfish	24½ x 17½
		La Pomme	Love's Awakening	11 x 8½
		Printemps	Springtime	
		Vieux Montmartre	Montmartre II, Charm of Montmartre	14½ x 21
		Voyages	Voyages	
	1933	La Dame Rose	Roses	11 x 8½
		Masque Noir	Masked	8½ x 13
		Modèle II	Modern Eve	16½ x 22
		Paravent Rouge	Unmasked	8½ x 13
		Les Roses	Belle Rose	21 x 17
		Sommeil	Repose	45 x 19
		Vitesse	Speed	25 x 15½
	1934	Grande Eve	Eve and the Serpent, Serpent and Apple	20 x 30
		Léda	Leda	31 x 21
		Les Lis	Lilies	19½ x 28
		Nageuse	Swimmer	31 x 21
		Poissons	Fish	25 x 18
		Quatuor	Melody Hour	23 x 18½
		Vacances	Summer Dreams	
	1935	Candeur	Winsome	15½ x 17½
		Can-Can Française	French Quadrille	25 x 15½
		Enigme	Sweet Mystery	16 x 20½-o
		Hop-la	Hop-la	11 x 8½
		Pivoines	Peonies	11 x 8½
		Repos	Ballerina	18½ x 14½
		Au Restaurant	Soda Fountain	11 x 16½
		Volupté	Ecstasy	15½ x 17½
	1936	A la Fête	Mardi Gras	18½ x 18½
		Au Bar	Gay Trio	11½ x 19½
		Berger et Bergère	Guardians	15" diameter
		Brébis et Agneau	The Favorite	15" diameter
		Le Coquillage	Song of the Sea	14½ x 18½
		Papillon I	Fluttering Butterfly	9 x 7
		Papillon II	Open Wings	9 x 7
		Papillon III	Woman in Wings	9 x 7
		Réveil	Pink Slippers	25 x 12
		La Source	Waterfall	8 x 20
		Symphonie en Bleu	Symphony in Blue	19½ x 23½
		Yachting	Yachting	24½ x 19

EDITION	DATE	FRENCH OR ORIGINAL TITLE	AMERICAN TITLE OR TITLES	SIZE
	1937	*Les Cygnes*	The Swans	
		Happy Birthday	Happy Birthday	18½ x 13½
		Le Jet d'Eau	The Fountain	8 x 20
		Miroir de Venise	Girl in Crinoline	19½ x 23½
		Les Orchidées	Orchids	19½ x 28
		Parfum de Fleurs	Love's Blossom	25 x 17
		Première Rose	Fair Model	11 x 18½
	1937	*Reflets*	The Pool	8 x 20
		Le Sofa	The Love Seat, The Sofa	25 x 17
	1938	*Aux Champs Elysées*	On the Champs Elysées	
		Corolles	Daydreams	
		Pur-sang	Thoroughbreds	35 x 18
		Rêve de Valse	Waltz Dreams	19 x 19
	1939	*L'Essayage*	The Pink Slip	11 x 19
		Fleurs de Nice	Spring Flowers	
		Gitane	Gay Senorita	21½ x 18
		Music Hall	Fair Dancer	22 x 19
	1940	*Falbalas*	Southern Charm	15 x 21
		Finlande!	Finlande!	21 x 14
		La Glycine	Wisteria	21 x 17½
		L'Invitée	Morning Cup	17½ x 19½
		Résonance	Waltz Echoes	17 x 14
		Sous le Toit	Attic Room	16½ x 14
		Tabac Blond	Illusion	9 x 19
	1941	*Arrivée*	Arrival	17 x 12-o
		Départ	Departure	17 x 12-o
	1946	*Au Bord de l'Eau*	At the Water's Edge	
		Bavardage (oil)	Gossip	
		Diner au Jardin (oil)	Dinner in the Garden	
		Intimité (oil)	Intimacy	
		Sommeil (oil)	Repose	
		Sous le Toit (oil)	Attic Room	
	1947	*Les Cygnes* (oil)	The Swans	
		En Calèche (oil)		
		Fin de Déjeuner (oil)	After Dinner	
	1948	*L'Amazone* (color reproduction of a drypoint)	Horsewoman	
	1948	*Frou-Frou*	Frou-Frou	
		La Lampe	The Pink Shade	19½ x 15½
		Rêve du Soir (drypoint)	Evening Dreams	
	1950	*Paris*	Paris	28½ x 20
	1953	*Promenade au Bois*	The Coach, Springtime Promenade	16 x 13

(copyrighted by Fanny
Icart. Etched by Louis
Icart in 1950.)

APPENDIX B

Louis Icart's illustrated books have been arranged by publication date. This listing, where possible, has included all elements of each volume—title, author, publisher, publication date, number and type of illustrations, typography, details of the edition as outlined in the *justification du tirage,* number of pages, and dimensions.

Names of papers used and other bibliographic terms are given in French. Definitions and additional details for each may be found in the glossary.

TITLE: *L'Ingénue Libertine*

AUTHOR: Colette Willy

PUBLISHER: Editions Excelsior, Paris

PUBLICATION DATE: 1926

ILLUSTRATIONS: 19 copperplate etchings, color

TYPOGRAPHY: Arrault & Cie.

EDITION: 1 example on *Papier de Chine,* 1 series of 25 drawings *inédités* in color

55 examples on *Japon Impérial.* 50 are numbered 1–50. 5 examples are *hors-commerce,* designated H.C.

65 examples on *Hollande Van Gelder.* 50 are numbered 51–100. 15 examples are *hors-commerce,* designated H.C.

425 examples on *Vergé à la forme de Rives.* 400 are numbered 101–500. 25 examples are *hors-commerce,* designated H.C.

PAGES: 191 pages

DIMENSIONS: page size, 10" x 13"

full-page plate size, 6" x 8½"

TITLE: *Bigarrure*

AUTHOR: Abel Hermant, de l'Académie Française

PUBLISHER: Les Images du Temps, Paris

PUBLICATION DATE: 1928

ILLUSTRATIONS: 10 woodcut initials and 6 etchings, black and color

1 etching by Madrassi

TYPOGRAPHY: Lapina

EDITION: 1 example on *Japon Impérial réimposé,* containing two signed, unpublished plates. Two states of the drypoints, one proof of the canceled plates, and one suite of illustrations in color. Designated No. 1

19 examples on *Vieux Japon* and two states of the drypoints. One proof of the canceled plate and one suite of illustrations in color on *Japon.* Designated No. 2–20

50 examples on *Japon Impérial réimposé.* Two states of drypoints. One proof of the canceled plate. One suite of illustrations in color. Nos. 21–70.

30 examples on *Japon Impérial réimposé*, Nos. 71–100

1,000 examples on *Vergé de Rives BFK pur chiffon*, Nos. 101–1100.

50 examples *hors-commerce* on diverse papers.

PAGES: 130

DIMENSIONS: page size, 5½″ x 7¾″.

full-page plate size, 3½″ x 5″.

TITLE: *Contemplations: La Fête chez Thérèse*

AUTHOR: Victor Hugo

PUBLISHER: Editions Excelsior, Paris

PUBLICATION DATE: 1930

ILLUSTRATIONS: copperplate etchings

TITLE: *Jean Niquet*

AUTHOR: Mme Jac d'Armaillot

PUBLISHER: Editions Jeune Peinture Française, Paris

PUBLICATION DATE: Christmas, 1934

ILLUSTRATIONS: by Icart, U. Brunellischi, A. Calbet, Francisque Poulbot, and E. M. Sandoz. Those by Louis Icart consist of six black and white illustrations for "Jean Niquet en Prison," pp. 41–56.

EDITION: 50 examples *hors-commerce* for the Christmas tree of Les Enfants des Artistes en Chômage de Nationalité Française et Italienne (Children of Unemployed French and Italian Artists).

200 examples, numbered in Roman characters, of which 75 copies are for the press and the remainder are gifts of the author.

20 examples are the property of the illustrators

500 examples, subscribed, to benefit Les Enfants des Artistes en Chômage de Nationalité Française et Italienne. Nos. 271–770.

This printing of *Jean Niquet* is the *édition originale*.

PAGES: 71

DIMENSIONS: plate sizes vary from 3″ x 4″ to 6″ x 4¼″

TITLE: *Don Quichotte de la Manche*

AUTHOR: Louis Icart

PUBLISHER: O. Schneider & Cie., Paris

PUBLICATION DATE: 1934

ILLUSTRATIONS: front- and back-cover illustration, original etching in black.

TYPOGRAPHY: O. Schneider & Cie., Paris

EDITION: 1 *exemplaire unique* on *Papier Japon*

20 examples on *Auvergne*, Nos. I–XX, *hors-commerce*

remainder of edition nonlimited.

PAGES: 252 pages

DIMENSIONS: page size, 5½″ x 8″

plate size, 3½″ x 5″

TITLE: *Le Sopha*

AUTHOR: Claude Prosper Jolyot de Crebillon (Crebillon *fils)*

PUBLISHER: Le Vasseur et Cie., Paris

PUBLICATION DATE: 1935

ILLUSTRATIONS: 23 original etchings, published at the presses of A. Porcaboeuf & Cie., Paris, employing *à la poupée* for coloring.

TYPOGRAPHY: Le Vasseur et Cie., Paris

EDITION: 22 examples on *Japon Impérial*. One original color composition, one sketch signed by the artist, one suite in black with engraved *remarques*, one gilded copperplate. Nos. 1–22

34 examples on *Hollande van Gelder,* one suite in black with engraved *remarques.* Nos. 23–57

443 examples on *Vélin de Rives,* watermarked with the name of Porcaboeuf et Cie. Nos. 58–497

DIMENSIONS: page size, 7½" x 9½"
plate size, 4½" x 6½"

TITLE: *Bug O'Shea*
AUTHOR: Paul Morand
PUBLISHER: Les Laboratoires Deglaude, Paris
PUBLICATION DATE: 1936
ILLUSTRATIONS: photomechanical-process illustrations, black and red. 8 full-page plates, 5 in-text plates
TYPOGRAPHY: Draeger Frères, Paris
EDITION: 5 examples on *Japon Impérial.* Nos. I–V
15 examples on *Hollande.* Nos. 6–20
remainder of edition nonlimited.
Original works for the illustrations are *hors-commerce,* reserved exclusively for "MM les Medicins"
PAGES: 89
DIMENSIONS: page size, 7" x 10"
plate size, 5½" x 7½"

TITLE: *Gargantua et Pantagruel*
AUTHOR: François Rabelais
PUBLISHER: Le Vasseur et Cie., Paris
PUBLICATION DATE: 1936
ILLUSTRATIONS: 76 photogravures, color
TYPOGRAPHY: Draeger Frères, Montrouge
EDITION: In 5 volumes, numbered I–V.

1 example on *Japon Super Nacré,* autographed by the artist, including one of the 76 original compositions which served for the illustrations; three sketches signed by the artist; six compositions *refusées,* originally intended for the free suite; one suite in black of the 76 plates, with *remarques* in black, in drypoint; the complete series of press proofs for the illustrations; one engraved and gilded copperplate. Designated No. 1

29 examples on *Japon Super Nacré,* autographed by the artist, including one of the 76 original compositions which served for the illustrations; one sketch signed by the artist; one composition *refusée;* one suite in black with remarques in drypoint; one engraved and gilded copperplate. Nos. 2–30

46 examples on *Japon Impérial,* including one of the 76 original compositions which served for the illustrations; one sketch signed by the artist; one suite of 76 plates in black with *remarques* in drypoint; one engraved and gilded copperplate. Nos. 31–76

900 examples on *Vélin d'Arches à la forme,* water-marked "Arches, Le Vasseur et Cie.," Nos. 77–976

DIMENSIONS: page size, 7½" x 9½"
plate size, 5¼" x 7¾"

TITLE: *La Dame aux Camélias*
AUTHOR: Alexandre Dumas *fils*
PUBLISHER: François Guillot, Paris
PUBLICATION DATE: 1938
ILLUSTRATIONS: 25 copperplate etchings
TYPOGRAPHY: J. Dumpulin, Paris.
Etchings printed by Manuel Robbe, Paris
EDITION: 25 examples on *Japon Super Nacré,* containing the etchings in color in their final state,

one suite in black, one original drawing, and one engraved plate

175 examples on *Vélin d'Arches à la forme,* which has been specially fabricated for this edition, including the etchings in color in their final state

Additional examples, on various papers, were published for the artist and printers.

PAGES: 247

DIMENSIONS: page size, 8¾" x 11¼"

plate size, 5¼" x 7½"

TITLE: *La Ronde des Danses—Kaléidoscope des "dancing" d'après-guerre*

AUTHOR: Léon Ruth

PUBLISHER: Charles Meunier, Paris

PUBLICATION DATE: 1938

ILLUSTRATIONS: 18 copperplate etchings

TYPOGRAPHY: Charles Meunier

EDITION: 150 examples on *Vélin d'Arches.* Nos. 1–150

PAGES: 48

DIMENSIONS: page size, 8½" x 11¼"

plate sizes vary, from 3" diameter to 6" x 7¼"

TITLE: *Le Sixième Mariage de Barbe-Bleue*

AUTHOR: Henri de Régnier

PUBLISHER: Le Vasseur et Cie., Paris

PUBLICATIONS DATE: 1938

ILLUSTRATIONS: 45 drypoints in black, originally conceived as monotypes

TYPOGRAPHY: Collaboration of Charles Meunier on the presses of the copperplate engraving printer, Alfred Porcabeuf et Cie., Paris

EDITION: 5 examples on *Japon Super Nacré,* including one drawing and one monotype signed by the artist; one suite of the engravings with *remarques;* one unprinted copperplate, gilded. Nos. 1–5

45 examples on handmade *Auvergne* paper, including one suite of engravings with *remarques;* one gilded copperplate. Nos. 6–50

150 examples printed on *Vélin Teinte de Rives.* Nos. 51–200

Additionally the *exemplaire unique,* having served for the edition of this work, executed entirely by the artist on *Vergé* paper made during the eighteenth century

DIMENSIONS: page size, 10" x 13"

plate size, 6½" x 9¾"

TITLE: *Don Quichotte de la Manche*

AUTHOR: Louis Icart

PUBLISHER: Les Editions Théâtrales, Paris

PUBLICATION DATE: 1938

ILLUSTRATIONS: None

TYPOGRAPHY: L'Imprimerie Planchier, Bonneville (Haute-Savoie)

EDITION: 1 *exemplaire unique* on *Hollande*

20 examples on *Japon,* Nos. I–XX, *hors-commerce*

PAGES: 270

DIMENSIONS: page size, 5½" x 8"

TITLE: *La Femme de Marbre*

AUTHOR: Henri de Régnier

PUBLISHER: privately printed on the presses of Alfred Porcabeuf et Cie.

PUBLICATION DATE:

ILLUSTRATIONS: 30 monotypes

TYPOGRAPHY: Charles Meunier, in collaboration with Alfred Porcabeuf et Cie.

EDITION: 1 *exemplaire unique,* dedicated to Fanny Icart
PAGES: 115
DIMENSIONS: page size, 9¾" x 13¼"
            plate size, 6" x 8"

TITLE: *Chrysis*
AUTHOR: Pierre Louÿs
PUBLISHER: Le Vasseur et Cie., Paris
PUBLICATION DATE: 1940
ILLUSTRATIONS: 15 color etchings
EDITION: 125 examples on *Vélin Crème*
            3 examples on *Vélin Blanc*
            4 examples on *Rives Teinte*
            15 examples on *Japon*
DIMENSIONS: page size, 8" x 11¼"
            plate size, 5¼" x 8"

TITLE: *Croquis de l'Exode*
AUTHOR: No text, conception by Louis Icart
PUBLISHER: Louis Icart
PUBLICATION DATE: 1940
ILLUSTRATIONS: 50 monotypes in black, green, and red.
EDITION: 1 *exemplaire unique,* dedicated to "Fanny, June 14–20"
PAGES: 50
DIMENSIONS: page size, 10" x 13"
            plate size, 6¼" x 8"

TITLE: *La Servitude Amoureuse de Juliette Drouet à Victor Hugo*
AUTHOR: Paul Souchon
PUBLISHER: Editions Albin Michel, Paris
PUBLICATION DATE: 1943
ILLUSTRATION: title page, in black, photomechanical reproduction
TYPOGRAPHY: Editions Albin Michel
EDITION: Non-limited
DIMENSIONS: illustration size, 3" x 2"

TITLE: *Léda ou La Louange des Bienheureuses Ténèbres*
AUTHOR: Pierre Louÿs
PUBLISHER: Le Vasseur et Cie., Paris
PUBLICATION DATE: 1943
ILLUSTRATIONS: 15 original etchings, color
TYPOGRAPHY: Under the direction of Charles Meunier, printed by Phillipe Renouard, Paris
EDITION: 1 example on *Japon,* with all the original drawings and sketches, signed, one original
            copperplate. Designated No. 1
            125 examples on *Vélin Crème*
            3 examples on *Vélin Blanc*
            3 examples on *Rives Teinte*
            15 examples on *Japon*
DIMENSIONS: page size, 8¼" x 11¼"
            plate size, 5½" x 8"

TITLE: *Faust*
AUTHOR: Johann Wolfgang von Goethe, translated by Gérard de Nerval
PUBLISHER: Le Vasseur et Cie., Paris

PUBLICATION DATE: 1944

ILLUSTRATIONS: 24 photogravures

TYPOGRAPHY: Draeger Frères

EDITION: In two volumes:

24 examples on *Vergé de Hollande* signed by the artist, including one of the original compositions for the work, one sketch signed by the artist, one suite of illustrations in black, one plate chromed and engraved. Nos. 1–24

400 examples on *Vélin d'Arches,* including one suite in color and one suite in black. Nos. 25–424

200 examples on *Vélin de Rives,* including one suite in black. Nos. 425–624

776 examples on *Vélin Alfa,* nos. 625–1400

53 examples for the artist and printers, *hors-commerce,* of which 7 are on *Vélin d'Arches à la forme,* nos. I–VII, and 46 are on *Vélin Alfa,* nos. VIII–LIII

DIMENSIONS: page size, 7½" x 9½"

plate size, 5¾" x 7¾"

TITLE: *La Vie des Seins*

AUTHOR: Docteur Jacobus, pseudonym for Louis Icart

PUBLISHER: Georges Guillot, Paris

PUBLICATION DATE: 1945

ILLUSTRATIONS: 15 original etchings, 15 *culs-de-lampes,* color

TYPOGRAPHY: Pierre Gaudin, Paris. Etchings printed on the presses of Manuel Robbe, Paris

EDITION: 10 examples on *Japon Super Nacré,* including one original drawing, states of the etchings, and one inked copperplate. Nos. 1–10

5 examples on *Japon,* including one original drawing, three states of etchings, one inked copperplate. Nos. 11–15

45 examples on *Japon,* with the etchings in color. Nos. 16–60

130 examples on *Arches,* with the etchings in color. Nos. 61–190

6 examples on *Japon,* reserved for the artist and publisher. Designated *Exemplaires d'artiste*

PAGES: 30

DIMENSIONS: page size, 8½" x 10"

plate size, single- and double-page spreads, no borders

TITLE: *Destin de Femme*

AUTHOR: Thérèse Castel

PUBLISHER: Editions Egix, Paris

PUBLICATION DATE: 1945

ILLUSTRATIONS: 21 original etchings, color

TYPOGRAPHY: Paul Zarifian

EDITION: *Edition Originale*

11 examples on *Hollande Pannekoeck,* including one original drawing, one engraved copperplate, one suite in color, one suite in black. Nos. 1–11

20 examples on *Vélin BFK,* including one suite in color, one suite in black. Nos. 12–31

125 examples on *Vélin BFK de Rives.* Nos. 32–156

139 examples on *Vélin Blanc.* Nos. 157–295

30 examples *hors-commerce,* reserved for the collaborators:

6 examples on *Hollande Pannekoeck.* Nos. I–VI

1 example on *Vélin BFK.* No. VII

23 examples on *Vélin Blanc.* Nos. VIII–XXX

PAGES: 154

DIMENSIONS: page size, 9¾" x 12¾"

full-page plate size, 7¾" x 10½"

partial-page plate size averages 6½" x 5"

TITLE: *La Nuit et Le Moment*
AUTHOR: Claude Prosper Jolyot de Crebillon (Crebillon *fils)*
PUBLISHER: Georges Guillot, Paris
PUBLICATION DATE: 1946
ILLUSTRATIONS: 25 color etchings
TYPOGRAPHY: Pierre Gaudin, etchings printed by Manuel Robbe
EDITION: 1 *exemplaire unique* on *Japon Super Nacré*, including 3 original drawings, one suite on *Chine* with three states of the etchings, the etchings in their final state, and one engraved copperplate. No. 1

15 examples on *Japon Impérial*, including 1 original drawing, two states of the etchings, one set of the etchings in their final state, and one engraved copperplate. Nos. 2–16

9 examples on *Japon Ivoire*, including one original drawing, two states of the etchings, one set of the etchings in their final state, and one engraved plate. Nos. 17–25

100 examples on *Rives à la forme*, including one original drawing, one suite in sanguine, and the etchings in their final state. Nos. 26–125

150 examples on *Arches à la forme*, including the etchings in their final state. Nos. 126–275

250 examples on *Johannot à la forme*, including the etchings in their final state. Nos. 276–525

15 examples on various papers, including the etchings in their final state, reserved for the artist and publisher. Indicated as *exemplaire d'artiste*. Nos. I–XV

PAGES: 163
DIMENSIONS: page size, 9¼" x 11½"
plate size, 5¼" x 7½"

TITLE: *Le Rêve*
AUTHOR: Emile Zola
PUBLISHER: Aux Editions du Livre, Monte Carlo
PUBLICATION DATE: 1946
ILLUSTRATIONS: offset reproduction—8 full page color, 8 black & white chapter heads
TYPOGRAPHY: Henri Kaeser, L'Imprimerie Centrale, Lausanne
EDITION: 3000 examples on Grand Vélin, #1–3000
PAGES: 220
DIMENSIONS: page size, 5½" x 7½"
plate size: 4" x 5¾"

TITLE: *Félicia ou Mes Fredaines*
AUTHOR: Andréa de Nerciat
PUBLISHER: Georges Guillot, Paris
PUBLICATION DATE: 1947
ILLUSTRATIONS: 20 etchings, color; 8 *culs-de-lampe*. Printed at the Studio of Manuel Robbe
TYPOGRAPHY: Joseph Zichieri
EDITION: 1 example on *Arches*, including the original watercolor for the frontpiece, three unpublished watercolors; one complete suite of etchings in color, artist signed; one suite in black; one suite in bistre on *Japon Impérial*. Designated No. 1

19 examples on *Arches*, including one original watercolor, one suite on *Japon Impérial* in black, one suite on *Japon Impérial* in *bistre*. Nos. 2–20

80 examples on *Arches*, including one original unpublished watercolor, one suite on *Japon Imperial*. Nos. 21–100

50 examples on *Arches*, including one suite in black. Nos. 101–150

450 examples on *Arches*. Nos. 151–500

30 examples reserved for the artist. Nos. I–XXX

PAGES: 188
DIMENSIONS: page size, 8¾" x 11"
plate size, 5¾" x 7¾"

TITLE: *Les Fleurs du Mal*
AUTHOR: Charles Baudelaire
PUBLISHER: Charles Meunier, Paris
PUBLICATION DATE: 1947
ILLUSTRATIONS: 108 stone lithographs
TYPOGRAPHY: Charles Meunier, type designed, composed, and printed by hand
EDITION: 1 example on *Japon Impérial* with one suite in sanguine before the addition of lettering. Contains one *cuir ciselé* by Charles Meunier. Signed title page. No. I
9 examples on *Arches*, including one *cuir ciselé* by Charles Meunier. Signed title page. Nos. II–X
10 examples on *Arches*. Signed title page. Nos. XI–XX
one *exemplaire unique*, on *Arches*, including the original wash drawings for the illustrations and one suite in black before the addition of type. Signed title page
PAGES: 127
DIMENSIONS: page size, 11" x 15¾"
plate size, 5½" x 7¼"

TITLE: *Chansons de Bilitis*
AUTHOR: Pierre Louÿs
PUBLISHER: Albin Michel, Paris
PUBLICATION DATE: 1949
ILLUSTRATIONS: 22 illustrations by Louis Icart, hand-colored by Albert Jon
EDITION: Second volume in a series of five selected works:
Vol. I *Aphrodite*, ill. by J. A. Conte
Vol. II *Chansons de Bilitis*, ill. by Louis Icart
Vol. III *La Femme et le Pantin*, ill. by J. Traynier
Vol. IV *Les Aventures du Roi Pausole*, ill. by de Beauville
Vol. V *Poèmes, Avant-propos de Yves Gerard le Dantec*, ill. by Berthomme Saint-André
20 examples on *Arches*, containing one suite in black, plus two original drawings for the series of 5 volumes
60 examples on *Pur Fil du Marais*, containing one suite in black, plus one drawing for the series of 5 volumes
150 examples on *Pur Fil Lafuma*, containing one suite in black
1,500 examples on *Vélin*
Only the last volume of the series bears the justifying numbers.
DIMENSIONS: page size, 7¼" x 9¼"
plate size, approximately the same, small margin

TITLE: *Les Amours de Psyché et de Cupidon*
AUTHOR: Jean de la Fontaine
PUBLISHER: Editions de la Cité
PUBLICATION DATE: 1949
ILLUSTRATIONS: 20 etchings, printed at studio of Manuel Robbe *fils*, 4 partial plates
TYPOGRAPHY: L'Imprimerie Nationale de France
EDITION: 20 examples on *Arches*, including one copperplate, the corresponding original drawing, one suite of all the illustrations in their first state and printed in black with *remarques*, one suite in the second state without remarques printed in sepia. No. 1–20.
30 examples on *Arches*, including one suite of the illustrations in the second state, printed in sepia. Nos. 21–50
100 examples on *Rives*, Nos. 51–150
An additional 15 examples have been printed out of commerce on *Lana* and designated for the artist and editors. Nos. I–XV.
PAGES: 240
DIMENSIONS: page size, 10" x 13¼"
plate size, 6½" x 9¼"

1. Susan Sontag, "Notes on 'Camp,'" *Against Interpretation* (New York: Farrar, Straus & Giroux, 1966), pp. 286-7.
2. Peyton Boswell, "Bedroom Paintings," *Art Digest,* September 1937, p. 14.
3. Jules Lafforgue, "Louis Icart, Peintre de Paris" (typescript).
4. Katharine Morrison McClinton, *Art Deco, A Guide for Collectors* (New York: Clarkson N. Potter, 1972), pp. 6-12.
5. François Fosca, *The Great Centuries of Painting,* transl. Stuart Gilbert (Geneva, Editions Albert Skira, 1952), p. 86.
6. Victor Emile Michelet, "Eugène Carrière," *Edouard Joseph Dictionnaire Biographique des Artistes Contemporains,* Tome I (Paris: Art & Edition, 1930), p. 244.
7. Jules Esquirol, "Louis Icart" (unpublished typescript), p. 3.
8. Esquirol, p. 3.
9. Esquirol, p. 5.
10. Esquirol, p. 9.
11. Esquirol, p. 7.
12. Esquirol, p. 12.
13. "Salon des Ironistes," *Le Cinacle* (Paris), November, 1912.
14. "La Salle Aeolian," *La Vie Intellectuelle* (Brussels), May 15, 1914.
15. Pierron Sander, *L'Indépendance Belge* (Brussels), February 16, 1914.
16. Esquirol, p. 11.
17. Pierre Albin, "A Ceux de l'Arrière," *Tous Les Journaux du Front* (Paris: Librairie Militaire Berger-Levrault, 1917), p. 7.
18. Louis Icart, "Comment On Fait un As," *Fantasio,* September 16, 1916, p. 157.
19. Pierre Lasseau (unpublished handwritten poem).
20. "Les Expositions," *La Voie Sacrée* (Paris), November, 1920.
21. *Le Matin* (Paris), March 9, 1920.
22. "L'Imagier," *L'Oeuvre* (Paris), March 7, 1920.
23. Hinyant, 1922 (unpublished handwritten poem).
24. Wanamaker's department store, catalog to the exhibition of Louis Icart's works, December/January, 1922-23.
25. "Louis Icart," The New York *Herald,* December 10, 1922.
26. "Sorel Hostess at Tea to Icart," New York *Telegraph,* December 10, 1922.

27. Ibid.
28. "Louis Icart," Audiberti (privately printed program).
29. Esquirol, p. 12.
30. Esquirol, p. 13.
31. "A Red Exhibition," *Daily Mail* (London), June 8, 1920.
32. R de B. "Les Théâtres," *L'Illustration* (Paris), November 4, 1933, p. 327.
33. *passim.*
34. "Le Cercle Molière a fait, au Casino Municipal, une création sensationnelle avec 'Don Quichotte' de M. Louis Icart," *Eclaireur du Soir* (Nice), April 25, 1938.
35. Gilbert Ponset, "Le peintre Louis Icart, auteur d'une nouvelle comédie sur 'Don Quichotte'," *Eclaireur du Soir* (Nice), April 22, 1938.
36. R. Bascher, *L'Illustration* (Paris), (letter to Louis Icart).
37. Letter to Louis Icart from "vos Locataires Allemands," July, 1940.
38. "Une Exposition du peintre Louis Icart," *Le Matin* (Paris), March 20, 1921.
39. Lucilius, "Chez le peintre Louis Icart," *Comoedia* (Paris), July 22, 1923.
40. Boswell, "Bedroom Paintings," p. 14.
41. Louis Icart, "The Technique of Etching," *Pictures and Decorations,* March 1, 1931, p. 27.
42. Ibid.
43. *Le Matin* (Paris), March 9, 1920.
44. *Daily Mail* (London), June 8, 1920.
45. *L'Oeuvre* (Paris), March 7, 1920.
46. Pierre Fontaine, "Carnet de Paris," *L'Auto* (Paris), March 13, 1942.
47. Ibid.
48. Ibid.
49. J. Quentin Riznik, *Daily Tribune* (New York), May 30, 1923.
50. Fontaine, "Carnet de Paris," March 13, 1942.
51. "Decorative White Visions," *Art Digest,* November 1, 1932.
52. Fontaine, "Carnet de Paris," March 13, 1942.
53. Esquirol, p. 17.
54. Los Angeles *Times,* December 20, 1948.
55. Louis Icart, *Le Voyage* (unpublished poem written on the back of the canvas *Le Voyage).*

GLOSSARY

The names and terms presented below are designed to aid the reader in a thorough understanding of the text. Some French terms, while they do not appear in this text may appear in the *Justification du Tirage* or *Achevé d'Imprimer* in certain *livres d'artistes* illustrated by Louis Icart. Their presentation here will guide collectors in determining the complete nature of a particular *livre d'artiste.*

A LA POUPÉE   A method of printing several colors simultaneously on one copperplate. The method employs separate pads or rolled felts to ink and wipe each color.

ACHEVÉ D'IMPRIMER   Located at the end of the *livre d'artiste,* it lists all the details concerning the production of the edition, such as printer's name, type styles used, date of printing. See *Justification du tirage.*

ALEXANDRINE   In poetry, a line of twelve or thirteen syllables. Rhymed *alexandrine* couplets are the classic form of French poetry.

AQUATINT   A method of intaglio etching in which a tonal resin or ground is applied to a copperplate, heated, and etched several times for tonal gradations and colors in multiple color intaglio work.

ARCHES   A pure rag paper from the paper mills of Arches in the Vosges region of France.

ARTIST'S PROOF   A proof copy of an autographically produced print, usually printed before final copies are readied and all the states have been finished.

AUVERGNE   A heavy pure rag paper from the Auvergne province in south central France.

BEAU LIVRE   See *livre d'artiste.*

BEAUX-ARTS   The fine arts: particularly, the École des Beaux-Arts in Paris which directed French artistic styles at the turn of the century.

BITING   A metal plate is inserted into an acid bath for a period of time sufficient to eat away lines that have been drawn in the ground.

LES BOCHES   A derogatory French term for the Germans, in use during World War I.

BURIN   An engraving tool, sometimes called a graver, for cutting metal plates in drypoint.

CHIAROSCURO   The alternate disposition of highlight and shadow in an oil painting or other work of art.

CHINE   Abbreviation for *Papier de Chine,* a thin strong paper made of bamboo shoots and other vegetable matter, generally of Oriental fabrication. Well suited to fine-line etching work.

COMMEDIA DELL'ARTE   A popular formal comedy that flourished in Italy from 1560 to 1625. The theatrical performances represented fauns, clowns, and mythical creatures that greatly influenced the eighteenth-century French painters.

CONTÉ CRAYON   A hard crayon made of graphite and clay, usually in red, gray, black, or other earth tones.

COPPERPLATE   A metal plate, sometimes made of zinc or aluminum, on which the etcher or engraver incises his image, either through the use of a burin or engraving needle or through an acid-biting process.

CUL-DE-LAMPE   A small design or picture drawn to conclude a chapter in a *livre d'artiste*.

DRYPOINT   See engraving.

EAU-FORTE   Etching.

EDITION D'ARTISTE   Edition of the artist. A special edition of the artist's work, reserved exclusively for his use and not for sale in most circumstances.

EDITION ORIGINALE   The first edition of the text as it appears in a *livre d'artiste*.

EN FEUILLES   The form in which most *livres d'artistes* are published, unbound in folded, unsewn sheets.

EN MARGE   In the margin.

EN TÊTE   An illustration at the head of a page, usually connected in some way to the immediate text.

ENGRAVING   An intaglio reproduction process, the act of cutting an image directly into a metal plate without the use of acids or grounds.

ETCHING   The act or process of making pictures on a metal plate by the corrosive action of acid instead of by a burin. The impression taken from an etched plate.

EXEMPLAIRE   Each copy of an edition, usually numbered.

EXEMPLAIRE DE TÊTE   In the *livre d'artiste*, special copies with some original feature such as the addition of original sketches.

FEATHERING   A technique in etching for biting only certain areas of a copperplate. Drops of acid are placed on areas of the plate and moved about with a feather or fine brush to achieve varying degrees of bite.

FÊTE CHAMPÊTRE   An outdoor festival or garden party.

FÊTES GALANTES   Characteristic outdoor festivals associated with the works of Jean Antoine Watteau, which generally feature elegantly attired figures in moments of peaceful idleness.

FILIGRANÉE   A watermark or a paper containing watermarks.

FOUR-COLOR REPRODUCTION   A photomechanical reproduction process which utilizes sensitized plates to produce colored halftone prints. Prints are easily identifiable under a magnifying glass because they reveal the necessary half-tone dot pattern or screen.

GRAVURE   A widely used French term for autographic illustrations of all types—etchings, lithographs, drypoints, etc.

GROUND   An acid-resistant covering which protects the etching plate. The image is incised into the ground and then immersed in an acid bath for biting. Grounds most commonly consist of two parts asphaltum, two parts beeswax, and one part powdered resin.

HALFTONE SCREEN   A regulated pattern of dots employed in photomechanical printing to permit reproductions of shades and colors.

HORS-COMMERCE   Books that are not for sale, special printings reserved for the artists or certain individuals.

HORS-TEXTE   A full-page illustration or illustration on a page without accompanying text.

IMPRESSION   A print from an inked block, stone, or plate.

IN-TEXTE   An illustration on a page in concert with some textual material.

INTAGLIO PROCESS   An incised or engraved design on a special plate made for reproduction purposes. Etching and aquatint are intaglio processes.

JAPON   Abbreviation of *Papier Japon*, a Dutch paper of fine and silky quality, well suited to fine-line etching work. Variations of this paper are *Japon Super Nacré* and *Japon Nacré*.

JUSTIFICATION DU TIRAGE   Similar to the English colophon in which all details about an edition of a book are indicated. Some of the same information may alternately be found in the *achevé d'imprimer*.

KITSCH   Objects, gestures, or styles that may be considered as bad taste, although somewhat amusing as well.

LETTRINE   A decorative capital initial, usually executed for a *livre d'artiste* by woodcut, linocut, or other intaglio method.

LITHOGRAPHIC STONE   A limestone or other calcerous substance on which the artist draws the image to be reproduced with a special lithographic crayon. Lithographs may also be photographically transferred to stones or special metal plates. See planograph.

LITHOGRAPHY   A planographic process in which prints are obtained from a stone on which an image has been drawn with a grease-based crayon.

LIVRE D'ARTISTE   A book whose illustrations are reproduced by an autographic reproduction process such as lithograph or etching as opposed to a photomechanical reproduction process. The book is considered a work of art and employs the combined talents of a master printer and an artist, known as a *peintre-graveur.*

LIVRE DE PEINTRE   Another name for the *livre d'artiste.*

LIVRE MANUSCRIT   A *livre d'artiste,* usually executed by one artist, in which both the book illustrations and the text are prepared via an autographic medium.

MAÎTRE D'OEUVRE   The person ultimately responsible for the co-ordination and outcome of the *livre d'artiste.*

MANIÈRE NOIRE   A technique in intaglio printing in which a wire brush or similar tool is passed in a pattern over a hard grounded plate surface. When etched, a lacy or similar pattern results on the impression.

MANIÈRE ROUGE   A term applied to the early canvases of Louis Icart in which tones of red and gold predominated.

MONOTYPE   The process and impression which results in a one-of-a-kind autographic print. Oils and inks are worked onto the surface of a glass or metal plate, then transferred directly to paper. Advantage of the method is that it allows for correction of the plate before printing. The method is also used by graphic artists as a "sketch" before etching a drawing on metal or drawing on lithographic stone.

PAPIER À MAIN   Handmade paper.

PEINTRE-GRAVEUR   The artist who executes the illustrations in a *livre d'artiste.*

PHOTOGRAVURE   An intaglio printing process in which works of art are photographically transferred to plates of copper or chrome, without the need for halftone screens.

PHOTO REPRODUCTION   A general term for any photographic processes used to reproduce illustrations or photographs. In printing, the four-color process employs halftone screens to achieve full-color effects.

PLANOGRAPHY   An artistic reproduction process, such as lithography, in which impressions are obtained from the surface of a stone or metal plate.

POCHOIR   A stencil reproduction process. The artist cuts a stencil, usually of brass, for each area of color in the design. Colors are then applied to the paper by hand by brushing through the openings in the stencil.

POILU   The French infantryman of the First World War. Literally translated, "the hairy one."

PROOF   An impression obtained from an inked block, plate, stone, or glass to determine its state.

REFUSÉ   A book illustration or group of illustrations that have been rejected by the artist and not included within the text. Such plates may, however, be included in suites.

REMARQUES   Small sketches or trials generally drawn into the bottom margins of etching plates. Such illustrations may be executed on the original copperplates or may later be added to the individual impressions in pencil or crayon.

RIVES   A make of paper used widely in the *livre d'artiste.* The paper has a smooth surface and is well-suited to fine-line illustrations.

LE SALON   The popular name for Le Société des Artistes Françaises, the "official" arm of French art, which wielded great influence in the 1800s. With the coming of the Impressionists, much of the *Salon's* power over artistic tastes faded, but the annual exhibits held significant influence throughout France prior to World War II. A salon, of course, refers to any gathering of a group of artists for purposes of exhibiting their works.

SERPENTE   A protective sheet of tissue found over copperplate engravings and etchings in some *livres d'artistes.*

SOFT-GROUND   An etching process in which Vaseline or tallow is added to the ground covering a metal plate. The ground remains semisoft and a variety of textures may be impressed into it, bitten into the plate, inked and printed.

STATE   A reworking of an etching plate or lithographic stone, whose various impressions constitute the stages of the work.

SUGAR LIFT   A tonal process in intaglio printing in which a sugar solution is painted onto areas of a copperplate covered with a ground. When bitten in acid, the sugar solution acts as a stopping agent, leaving the impressions desired by the artist.

SUITE   A series of illustrations supplied at the back of the *livre d'artiste,* apart from the text, which may include duplicates of those same illustrations. Suites often feature certain variations such as different paper stocks, use of colors, additions of *remarques.* Additional illustrations that do not appear within the body of the work may also be included in the suite.

TAILLE-DOUCE   Printing from copperplate, engraving, etchings.

TIRAGE   The number of copies in the edition of the *livre d'artiste.* Generally outlined in the *justification du tirage* or *achevé d'imprimer.*

VÉLIN   A woven paper made from pure rag. Several manufacturers' products such as *Vélin d'Arches* and *Vélin du Marais* are widely used by graphic artists.

VERGÉ   A type of laid paper, showing characteristic "laid" lines, parallel marks which are a result of the paper-molding process.

VERNISSAGE   A preview of an art exhibit or prepublication of a *livre d'artiste.*

LES VISIONS BLANCHES   "White Visions" is the name attributed to the series of oils created by Louis Icart in the 1930s and 1940s.

SELECTED BIBLIOGRAPHY

BOOKS

Battersby, Martin. *The Decorative Twenties*. New York: Walker & Co., 1969.

Bland, David. *A History of Book Illustration*. London: Farber and Farber, Ltd., 1958.

Carline, Richard. *Pictures in the Post*. London: Gordon Fraser, 1971.

Copplestone, Trewin, and Meyers, Bernard., eds. *Art Treasures in France*. New York: McGraw-Hill Book Company, and London: Hamlyn Publishing Group, Ltd., 1969.

Edouard-Joseph, *Dictionnaire Biographique des Artistes Contemporains, 1910–30*, vol. 3. Paris: Art & Edition, 1930.

Fosca, François. *The Eighteenth Century: Watteau to Tiepolo, The Great Centuries of Painting*. Translated by Stuart Gilbert. Geneva: Editions Albert Skira, 1952.

Gardner, Helen. *Gardner's Art Through the Ages*, 5th ed. Revised by Horst de la Croix and Richard G. Tansey. New York: Harcourt, Brace & World, Inc., 1970.

Garvery, Eleanor M., and Wick, Peter A. *The Arts of the French Book: 1900–1965*. Dallas: Southern Methodist University Press, 1967.

La Grande Guerre par les Artistes. Paris: Librairie Militaire Berger-Levrault, 1918.

Heller, Jules. *Printmaking Today: An Introduction to the Graphic Arts*. New York: Holt, Rinehart and Winston, 1958.

Hillier, Bevis. *Art Deco*. New York: E. P. Dutton and Co., 1969.

Laffont-Bompiani. *Dictionnaire des Oeuvres de tous les temps et de tous les pays*. Paris: Société d'édition de dictionnaires et encyclopédies, 1962.

Lucie-Smith, Edward. *A Concise History of French Painting*. New York: Praeger Publishers, 1971.

Mayer, Ralph. *The Artist's Handbook of Materials and Techniques*, 3rd ed., New York: The Viking Press, 1970.

McClinton, Katharine M. *Art Deco: A Guide for Collectors*. New York: Clarkson N. Potter, Inc., 1972.

Pool, Phoebe. *Impressionism*. New York/Washington: Praeger Publishers, Inc., 1967.

Rasmussen, Valdras, ed. *Catalogue Valdras 1934, Repertoire alphabétique des ouvrages français publié au cours de l'année*. Paris, 1935.

Romano, Clare, and Ross, John. *The Complete Printmaker*. New York: The Free Press, 1972.

Sontag, Susan, "Notes on Camp." *Against Interpretation*. New York: Farrar, Straus & Giroux, 1966.

Staff, Frank. *The Picture Postcard and Its Origins*. London: Lutterworth Press, 1966.

Strachan, W. J. *The Artist and the Book in France*. London: Peter Owen Ltd., 1969.

Thuillier, Jacques. *Fragonard*. Translated by Robert Allen. Geneva: Editions d'Art Albert Skira, 1967.

Tous les Journaux du Front. Paris: Librairie Militaire Berger-Levrault, 1917.

Weitenkampf, Frank. *The Illustrated Book*. Cambridge: Harvard University Press, 1938.

ARTICLES

A.,Ch. "L'Oeuvre du peintre Louis Icart." *Beaux-Arts* (Paris), June 1921.

"Un Artiste Français." *Courrier des Etats-Unis* (Paris), 4 December 1922.

"Les Arts." *La Scène* (Paris), 25 February 1921.

"Les Arts: L'exposition du peintre Louis Icart." *La Scène* (Paris), 26 March 1921.

Des Bois, Pierre. "Les Livres: La Tragédie de la Route." *L'Auto* (Paris), 27 January 1943.

Boswell, Peyton. "Bedroom Paintings." *Art Digest*, September 1937, p. 3.

Calel, Pierre. "Mon Cher Ami," *La Voie Sacrée* (Paris), January 1921.

De Contamin, P. "L'exposition Louis Icart." *Le Mecerre* (Paris), April 1921.

"Decorative White Visions: Exhibit—Metropolitan Galleries." *Art Digest,* 1 November 1932, p. 14.

"Dessinateurs-Humoristes," *Masques et Visages* (Paris), 4 April 1914.

"L'Echo des Gourbis." *Indépendance Belge* (Brussels), 12 March 1918.

"L'Echo des Gourbis." *Le Midi au Front* (Paris), 25 May 1916.

"Etcher Uses Trademark to Foil Piracy." *Art Digest,* 15 January 1932, p. 22.

"Les Expositions." *La Nation Belge* (Brussels), 6 March 1922.

"Les Expositions." *La Voie Sacrée* (Paris), November 1920.

"Une exposition aux Galéries d'art G. L. Manuel Frères." *Le Matin* (Paris), 4 March 1921.

"Une Fête de l'Élégance." *Comoedia* (Paris), 24 March 1922.

"La Guerre et les Humoristes." *Liberté* (Paris), 29 April 1917.

Honoré, Léopold. "11e Salon de la Gravure Originale en Couleurs." *Journal des Arts* (Paris), 22 December 1920.

"Icart Paintings Shown." *Art Digest,* 1 April 1932, p. 13.

L. M. "Vision d'art: La Gravure Originale en Couleurs." *Le Gaulois* (Paris), 1 November 1913.

"L'Imagier." *L'Oeuvre* (Paris), 7 March 1920.

"Louis Icart, Noted for his Etchings, Visits Friends in U.S." *Picture and Gift Journal,* December 1948, pp. 12–13.

"Louis Icart: Obituary." *Art Digest,* 1 March 1951, p. 31.

Lucilius, "Chez le peintre Louis Icart." *Comoedia* (Paris), 22 July 1923.

J. M. "Arts, Sciences, Lettres: Louis Icart." *Libre Belgique* (Brussels), 9 March 1922.

"La Mode par les Artistes." *L'Opinion* (Paris), 17 April 1920.

Morro, Clement. "Louis Icart." *La Revue Moderne* (Paris), June 1921.

"Nos Artistes." *La Dépêche de Toulouse* (Toulouse), 7 March 1920.

"Nos Compatriotes." *La Dépêche de Toulouse* (Toulouse), 23 May 1914.

Osborne, Carol. "Impressionists and the Salon." *Arts Magazine,* June 1974, pp. 36–39.

Pezeu, Charles. "Deux Toulousians, peintres de Parisiennes." *Le Télégramme* (Toulouse), 21 July 1920.

Ponset, Gilbert. "Le Peintre Louis Icart: auteur d'une nouvelle comédie sur 'Don Quichotte.' " *Eclaireur du Soir* (Nice), 22 April 1938.

Raybaut, Aline. "Le Cercle Molière de Nice de faire une très importante création, Don Quichotte de la Manche." *Le Théâtre Amateur* (Nice), November 1938.

"A Red Exhibition." *Daily Mail* (London), 8 June 1920.

Rey, Robert. "Lettre ouverte à M. Flandrin." *L'Opinion* (Paris), 13 March 1921.

"Le Ruban Rouge: Louis Icart." *Telegramme* (Toulouse), 26 February 1927.

"Salle Aeolian: Exposition Louis Icart." *La Gazette de Chaleroi* (Brussels), 25 February 1914.

"Salon des Ironistes." *Le Cinacle* (Paris), November 1912.

Sander, Pierron. *L'Indépendance Belge* (Brussels), 16 February 1914.

"Sorel Hostess at Tea to Icart." New York *Telegraph,* 10 December 1922.

Veran, Jules. "L'Exposition Louis Icart à la Haye." *Le Provençal de Paris,* 8 May 1922.

Veve, Docteur. "Le Poilu: un peintre d'aujourdhui, Louis Icart." *L'Ame Gauloise* (Paris), 17 July 1921.

Veve, Docteur. "Louis Icart." *Le Poilu* (Paris), May 1921.

La Vie Intellectuelle (Brussels), 15 May 1914.

"Voici l'Echo des Gourbis." *Presse* (Paris), 27 September 1916.

Wilhelm, Jacques. "Fragonard-illustrateur." *Le Portique* (Paris), No. 1 (1945), p. 91.

MANUSCRIPTS

Audiberti, "Louis Icart." Typescript. Private collection.

Esquirol, Jules. "Louis Icart." Typescript. Private collection.

Lafforgue, Jules. "Louis Icart: Peintre de Paris." Typescript. Private collection.

CATALOGUES AND PROGRAMS

"Don Quichotte de la Manche." Program: *Casino Municipal de Nice,* 23 April 1938.

"La Guerre et les Humoristes: catalogue illustré." *La Société des dessinateurs-humoristes et la Société des artistes-humoristes,* Paris, 1917.

The letter *L* after a title indicates that it is a *livre d'artiste*, illustrated by Louis Icart. The letter *E* after a title indicates that it is an etching. *Italic* page numbers indicate illustrations. Except where noted, works shown were done by Louis Icart. Titles of works are generally listed with the French title first.